We got very good at burning shoe boxes. We crayoned windows, cut doors on the sides, and dropped ants into the boxes, imagining they were people wanting very badly to live. Once the fire got going, I wailed like a siren and Rick flicked water from a coffee can at the building leaping with flames. More often than not, it burned to ash and the ants shriveled to nothing—though a few would limp away, wiser by vision of death.

LIVING UP THE STREET:

Narrative Recollections

Gary Soto

Strawberry Hill Press

Copyright © 1985 by Gary Soto
Strawberry Hill Press
2594 15th Avenue
San Francisco, California 94127

Proofread by Eric Baxter

Cover Art by Rick Soto

Typeset by Cragmont/Ex-Press, Oakland, California

Printed by Edwards Brothers, Inc., Ann Arbor, Michigan

Manufactured in the United States of America

Second printing, 1986

Library of Congress Cataloging in Publication Data

Soto, Gary.
    Living up the street.

    Summary: The author describes his experiences growing up as a Mexican American in Fresno, California.
    1. Soto, Gary. 2. Mexican Americans—California—Fresno—Biography. 3. Fresno (Calif.)—Biography.
[1. Mexican Americans—Biography] I. Title.
F869.F8S67 1985 979.4'830046872073 [92] 85-9893
ISBN 0-89407-064-9 (pbk.)

ACKNOWLEDGMENTS

"Getting By" first appeared in *Telescope*. "1, 2, 3" first appeared in *Revista Chicano-Riquena*.

I wish to express my gratitude to Chris Buckley, who read parts of this book, and to my wife, who read the entire book over and over until it looked right.

This book is for Rick, Debra, Little John, and Scott—the people who lived these stories.

Contents

Being Mean

We were terrible kids, I think. My brother, sister, and I felt a general meanness begin to surface from our tiny souls while living on Braly Street, which was in the middle of industrial Fresno. Across the street was Coleman Pickles, while on the right of us was a junkyard that dealt in metals—aluminum, iron, sheet metal, and copper stripped from refrigerators. Down the street was Sun-Maid Raisin, where a concrete tower rose above the scraggly sycamores that lined Braly Street. Many of our family worked at Sun-Maid: Grandfather and Grandmother, Father, three uncles, an aunt, and even a dog whose job was to accompany my grandfather, a security guard, on patrol. Then there was Challenge Milk, a printing shop, and the 7-Up Company where we stole sodas. Down the alley was a broom factory and Western Book Distributor, a place where our future step-father worked at packing books into cardboard boxes, something he would do for fifteen years before the company left town for Oregon.

This was 1957. My brother Rick was six, I was five, and Debra was four. Although we looked healthy, clean in the morning, and polite as only Mexicans can be polite, we had a streak of orneriness that we imagined to be normal play. That summer—and the summer previous—we played with the Molinas who lived down the alley from us right across from the broom factory and its brutal "whack" of straw being tied into brooms. There were eight children on the block that year, ranging from twelve down to one, so there was much to do: Wrestle, eat raw bacon, jump from the couch, sword fight with rolled-up newspapers, steal from neighbors, kick chickens, throw rocks at passing cars.... While we played in the house, Mother Molina just watched us run around, a baby in her arms crying like a small piece of machinery turning at great speed. Now and then she would warn us with a smile, "Now you kids, you're going to hurt yourselves." We ignored her and went on pushing one another from an opened window, yelling wildly when we hit the ground because we imagined that there was a school of sharks ready to snack on our skinny legs.

What we learned from the Molinas was how to have fun, and what we taught them was how to fight. It seemed that the Sotos were inherently violent. I remember, for instance, watching my aunts going at one another in my grandmother's back yard, while the men looked on with beers in their hands and mumbled to one another, perhaps noting the beauty of a jab or a roundhouse punch. Another time the police arrived late at night in search of our Uncle Leonard who had gotten into a fight at a neighborhood bar. Shortly thereafter, I recall driving with my mother to see him at what she said was a "soldier's camp." She had a sack of goods with her, and after speaking softly to a uniformed man we were permitted to enter. It was lunch time and he sat on a felled log laughing with other men. When he saw us coming, he laughed even harder.

In turn, I was edged with a meanness; and more often than not the object of my attacks was Rick. If upset, I chased him with rocks, pans, a hammer, whatever lay around in the yard. Once, when he kicked over a row of beans I had planted in the yard, I chased him down the alley with a bottle until, in range, I hurled it at him. The bottle hit him in the thigh and, to my surprise, showered open with blood. Screaming, his mouth open wide enough to saucer a hat inside, he hobbled home while I stood there, only slightly worried at his wound and the spanking that would follow, shouting that he had better never do that again. And he didn't.

I was also hurt by others who were equally as mean, and I am thinking particularly of an Okie kid who yelled that we were dirty Mexicans. Perhaps so, but why bring it up? I looked at my feet and was embarrassed, then mad. With a bottle I approached him slowly in spite of my brother's warnings that the kid was bigger and older. When I threw the bottle and missed, he swung his stick and my nose exploded blood for several feet. Frightened, though not crying, I ran home with Rick and Debra chasing me, and dabbed at my face and T-shirt, poked mercurochrome at the tear that bubbled, and then lay on the couch, swallowing blood as I slowly grew faint and sleepy. Rick and Debra looked at me for a while, then got up to go outside to play.

Rick and I and the Molinas all enjoyed looking for trouble and often went to extremes to try to get into fights. One day we found ourselves staring at some new kids on the street—three of them about our age—and when they looked over their picket fence to see who we were, I thought one of them had sneered at us, so I called him a name. They called back at us, and that provocation was enough to send Rick to beat on one of them. Rick entered their yard and was punched in the ear, then in the back when he tried to hunch over to protect himself. Furious as a bee, I ran to fight the kid who had humbled Rick, but was punched in the stomach, which knocked the breath out of me so I couldn't tell anyone how much it had hurt. The Molinas grew scared and ran home, while Rick and I, slightly roughed up but sure that we had the guts to give them a good working over, walked slowly home trying to figure out how to do it. A small flame lit my brain, and I suggested that we stuff a couple of cats into potato sacks and beat the kids with them. An even smaller light flared in my brother's brain. "Yeah, that'll get them," he said, happy that we were going to get even. We called to our cat, Boots, and found another unfortunate cat that was strolling nonchalantly down our alley in search of prime garbage. I called to it, and it came, purring. I carried it back to our yard where Rick had already stuffed Boots into a sack, which was bumping about on the ground. Seeing this, the cat stiffened in my arms and I had trouble working the cat into the sack, for it had spread its feet and opened its claws. But once inside, the cat grew calm, resigning itself to fate, and meowed only once or twice. For good measure I threw a bottle into my sack, and the two of us—or, to be fair, the four of us—went down the alley in search of the new kids.

We looked for them, even calling them names at their back porch, but they failed to show themselves. Rick and I believed that they were scared, so in a way we were victors. Being mean, we kicked over their garbage cans and ran home where we fought one another with the sacks, the cats all along whining and screaming to get out.

Perhaps the most enjoyable summer day was when Rick, Debra, and I decided to burn down our house. Earlier in the summer we had watched a television program on fire prevention at our grandmother's house, only three houses down from us on Sarah Street. The three of us sat transfixed in front of the gray light of the family's first TV. We sat on the couch with a bowl of grapes, and when the program ended the bowl was still in Rick's lap, untouched. TV was that powerful.

Just after that program Rick and I set fire to our first shoe box, in which we imagined were many people scurrying to get out. We hovered over the fire, and our eyes grew wild. Later, we got very good at burning shoe boxes. We crayoned windows, cut doors on the sides, and dropped ants into the boxes, imagining they were people wanting very badly to live. Once the fire got going, I wailed like a siren and Rick flicked water from a coffee can at the building leaping with flames. More often than not, it burned to ash and the ants shriveled to nothing—though a few would limp away, wiser by vision of death.

But we grew bored with the shoe boxes. We wanted something more exciting and daring, so Rick suggested that we brighten our lives with a house fire. "Yeah," Debra and I cried, leaping into the air, and proceeded to toss crumpled newspapers behind the doors, under the table, and in the middle of the living room. Rick struck a match, and we stood back laughing as the flames jumped wildly about and the newspaper collapsed into ash that floated to the ceiling. Once the fire got started we dragged in the garden hose and sprayed the house, the three of us laughing for the love of good times. We were in a frenzy to build fires and put them out with the hose. I looked at Rick and his eyes were wide with pleasure, his crazed laughter like the mad scientists of the movies we would see in the coming years. Debra was jumping up and down on the couch, a toy baby in her arms, and she was smiling her tiny teeth at the fire. I ran outside flapping my arms because I wanted to also burn the chinaberry that stood near our bedroom window. Just as I was ready to set a match to a balled newspaper I intended to hurl into the branches, our grandmother came walking slowly down the alley to check on us. (It was her responsibility to watch us during the day because our father was working at Sun-Maid Raisin and our mother was peeling potatoes at Reddi-Spud.) Grandma stopped at the gate and stared at me as if she knew what we were up to, and I stared back so I could make a quick break if she should lunge at me. Finally she asked, "How are you, honey?" I stared at my dirty legs, then up to her: "OK. I'm just playing." With the balled newspaper in my hand, I pointed to the house and told her that Rick and Debra were inside coloring. Hearing this she said to behave myself, gave me a piece of gum, and returned to her house.

When I went back inside Rick and Debra were playing war with cherry tomatoes. Debra was behind the table on which the telephone rested, while Rick crouched behind a chair making the sounds of bombs falling.

"Rick," I called because I wanted to tell him that Grandma had come to see how we were doing, but he threw a tomato and it splashed my T-shirt like a bullet wound. I feigned being shot and fell to the floor. He rolled from behind the chair to hide behind a door. "Are you dead?" he asked. I lifted my head and responded: "Only a little bit."

Laughing, we hurled tomatoes at one another, and some of them hit their mark—an ear, a shoulder, a grinning face—while others skidded across the floor or became pasted to the wall. "You Jap," Debra screamed as she cocked her hand to throw, to which I screamed, "You damn German." We fought laughing until the tomatoes were gone. Breathing hard, we looked at the mess we had created, and then at each other, slightly concerned at what it might mean. Rick and I tried to clean up with a broom while Debra lay exhausted on the couch, thumb in her mouth and making a smacking sound. I can't recall falling asleep but that's what happened, because I awoke to Rick crying in the kitchen. Our mother had come home to an ash-darkened living room, a puddled kitchen, and tomato-stained walls. She yelled and spanked Rick, after which she dragged him to the stove where she heated a fork over a burner and threatened to burn his wrists. "Now are you going to play with fire?" she screamed. I peeked into the kitchen and her mouth was puckered into a dried fruit as Rick cried that she was hurting him, that he was sorry, that he would never do it again. Tears leaped from his face as he tried to wiggle free. She threw the fork into the sink, then let him go. She turned to me and yelled: "And you too, *Chango!*" She started after me, but I ran out the front door into the alley where I hid behind a stack of boards. I stayed there until my breathing calmed and my fear disappeared like an ash picked up by the wind. I got up and, knowing that I couldn't return home immediately, I went to the Molinas. Just as I turned into their yard I caught sight of two of them climbing, hand over hand, on the telephone wires that stretched from above the back porch to the pole itself. A few of the younger Molinas looked on from an opened window, readying for their turn, as the radio blared behind them. I threw a rock at the two hanging from the wires, and they laughed that I missed. The other kids laughed. Their mother, with a baby in her arms, came out to the back porch, laughed, and told us to behave ourselves.

Father

My father was showing me how to water. Earlier in the day he and a friend had leveled the backyard with a roller, then with a two-by-four they dragged on a rope to fill in the depressed areas, after which they watered the ground and combed it slowly with a steel rake. They were preparing the ground for a new lawn. They worked shirtless in the late summer heat, and talked only so often, stopping now and then to point and say things I did not understand—how fruit trees would do better near the alley and how the vegetable garden would do well on the east side of the house.

"Put your thumb like this," he said. Standing over me, he took the hose and placed his thumb over the opening so that the water streamed out hissing and showed silver in that dusk. I tried it and the water hissed and went silver as I pointed the hose to a square patch of dirt that I soaked but was careful not to puddle.

Father returned to sit down with an iced tea. His knees were water-stained and his chest was flecked with mud. Mom sat next to him, garden gloves resting on his lap. She was wearing checkered shorts and her hair was tied up in a bandana. He patted his lap, and she jumped into it girlishly, arms around his neck. They raised their heads to watch me—or look through me, as if something were on the other side of me—and talked about our new house—the neighbors, trees they would plant, the playground down the block. They were tired from the day's work but were happy. When Father pinched her legs, as if to imply they were fat, she punched him gently and played with his hair.

The water streamed, nickel-colored, as I slowly worked from one end to the next. When I raised my face to Father's to ask if I could stop, he pointed to an area that I had missed. Although it was summer I was cold from the water and my thumb hurt from pressing the hose, trigger-like, to reach the far places. But I wanted to please him, to work hard as he had, so I watered the patch until he told me to stop. I turned off the water, coiled the hose as best I could, and sat with them as they talked about the house and stared at where I had been standing.

The next day Father was hurt at work. A neck injury. Two days later he was dead. I remember the hour—two in the afternoon. An uncle slammed open the back door at Grandma's and the three of us—cousin Isaac, Debbie, and I who were playing in the yard—grew stiff because we thought we were in trouble for doing something wrong. He looked at us, face lined with worry and shouting to hurry to the car. At the hospital I recall Mother holding her hand over her eyes as if she was looking into a light. She was leaning into someone's shoulder and was being led away from the room in which Father lay.

I remember looking up but saying nothing, though I sensed what had happened—that Father was dead. I did not feel sorrow nor did I cry, but I felt conspicuous because relatives were pressing me against their legs or holding my hand or touching my head, tenderly. I stood among them, some of whom were crying while others had their heads bowed and mouths moving. The three of us were led away down the hall to a cafeteria where an uncle bought us candies that we ate standing up and looking around, after which we left the hospital and walked into a harsh afternoon light. We got into a blue car I had never seen before.

At the funeral there was crying. I knelt with my brother and sister, hands folded and trying to be patient, though I was itchy from the tiny coat whose shoulders worked into my armpits and from the heat of a stuffy car on our long and slow drive from the church in town. Prayers were said and a eulogy was given by a man we did not know. We were asked to view the casket, with our mother and the three of us to lead the procession. An uncle helped my mother while we walked shyly to view our father for the last time. When I stood at the casket, I was surprised to see him, eyes closed and moist-looking and wearing a cap the color of skin. (Years later I would realize that it hid the wound from which he had died.) I looked quickly and returned to my seat, head bowed because my relatives were watching me and I felt scared.

We buried our father. Later that day at the house, Grandma could not stop shaking from her nerves, so a doctor was called. I was in the room when he opened his bag and shiny things gleamed from inside it. Scared, I left the room and sat in the living room with my sister, who had a doughnut in her hand, with one bite gone. An aunt whose face was twisted from crying looked at me and, feeling embarrassed, I lowered my head to play with my fingers.

A week later relatives came to help build the fence Father had planned for the new house. A week after that Rick, Debra, and I were playing in an unfurnished bedroom with a can of marbles Mother had given us. Behind the closed door we rolled the marbles so that they banged against the baseboard and jumped into the air. We separated, each to a corner, where we swept them viciously with our arms—the clatter of the marbles hitting the walls so loud I could not hear the things in my heart.

1, 2, 3

When I was seven years old I spent most of the summer at Romain playground, a brown stick among other brown kids. The playground was less than a block from where we lived, on a street of retired couples, Okie families, and two or three Mexican families. Just before leaving for work our mother told us—my brother Rick, sister Debra, and me—not to leave the house until after one in the afternoon, at which time I skipped off to the playground, barefoot and smiling my teeth that were uneven and without direction. By that hour the day was yellow with one-hundred-degree heat, the sun blaring high over the houses. I walked the asphalt street with little or no pain toward a mirage of water that disappeared as I approached it.

At the playground I asked for checkers at the game room, unfolded the board under the elm that was cut with initials and, if he was there, I played with Ronnie, an Okie kid who was so poor that he had nothing to wear but a bathing suit. All summer he showed up in his trunks, brown as the rest of us Mexicans, and seemed to enjoy himself playing checkers, Candyland, and Sorry. Once, when I brought him an unwrapped jelly sandwich in my hand, the shapes of my fingers pressed into the bread, he took it and didn't look into my eyes. He ate very slowly, deliberating over each move. When he beat me and had polished off his sandwich, he turned away without a word and ran off to play with someone else.

If Ronnie was not there and no one else challenged me, I just sat under the tree stacking checkers until they toppled over and I started again to raise that crooked spine of checkers a foot high.

If there were only little kids—four or five-year-olds who could count to ten—I played Candyland, a simple game of gum drops and sugar canes down a road to an ice cream sandwich. I remember playing with Rosie, a five-year-old whose brother Raymond got his leg broken when he was hit by a car. I was not around that day, but I recall racing a friend to where it had happened to look at the dried blood on the curb. My friend and I touched the stain. I scratched at it so that a few flakes got under my nails, and no matter how I picked and sucked at them, they wouldn't come out. We both ran home very frightened.

Rosie sat across the picnic-like table from me, her stringy hair spiked with a few flowers, and called me "Blackie" when it was my turn to spin the wheel and move down the candyland road. I didn't hit her because she had six brothers, five of them bigger than me. To smack her would have meant terror that would last for years. But the truth was that she liked me, for she offered me sunflower seeds from her sweaty palms and let me spit the shells at her.

"Spin the wheel Blackie," she said with a mouthful of her seeds and sniffling from a perennial cold, a bubble of snot coming and going.

"OK, tether-ball-head," I countered. Both of us laughed at each other's cleverness while we traded off spitting shells at one another, a few pasting themselves to our foreheads.

One Saturday morning a well-dressed man let his daughter try the slide. Rosie ran over to join the little girl, who was wearing a dress, her hair tied into a neat pony tail. Her shoes were glossy black and she wore socks with red trim. Rosie squealed at the little girl and the girl squealed back, and they both ran off to play while the father sat with his newspaper on the bench.

I went and sat on the same bench, shyly picking at the brittle, green paint but not looking up at the man at first. When my eyes did lift, slowly like balloons let go, I took it all in: His polished shoes, creased pants, the shirt, and his watch that glinted as he turned the page of his newspaper. I had seen fathers like him before on the *Donna Reed Show* or *Father Knows Best*, and I was pleased that he was here at *our* playground because I felt that we were being trusted, that nearby, just beyond our block, the rich people lived and were welcoming.

He looked up from the newspaper at me and forced a quick

smile that relaxed back into a line as he returned to his paper. Happily I jumped from the bench and rushed to play with Rosie and the little girl, hoping to catch the man's eye as I swung twice as high as the girls and parachuted with great abandon to land like a frog. He looked up to smile, but dropped his eyes back to the newspaper as he recrossed his legs.

But then it happened: The little girl fell from the swing while Rosie was pushing her. Startled by her sudden crying, the man's eyes locked on the scene of Rosie hovering over his daughter crying on the ground. He jumped up yelling, "You filthy Mexican." He picked up his daughter who had stopped crying, and then, turning to Rosie who was saying that she hadn't done anything, he shoved her hard against the chain link fence so that her sunflower seeds flew in every direction. She got up bent over, her breath knocked out, mouth open wide as a cup and a string of saliva lengthening to the ground.

Three of her brothers were playing Chinese checkers under the tree, and when they saw what had happened they ran to fight the man with handfuls of redwood chips that they had scooped up from the play area. Like the rest of us, the brothers, who ranged from eight to fourteen, wore T-shirts and cut-offs but with no shoes—sons of the very poor. But unlike the rest of us, they were fierce brawlers who would go at it even with older kids as they flew up like chickens against those who got them mad.

Yelling, "You nigger people," his raised arm blocking the puffs of redwood chips, the man was backed into the merry-go-round while his daughter, some distance away, clung to the chain link fence. He charged one brother and pushed him to the ground only to feel a handful of redwood chips against his face. Coughing, he grabbed another brother and threw him to the ground while still another threw a softball at his back. In pain, the man turned around and chased the brother, but was stopped by the coach who had come running from the baseball game on the other side of the playground.

"Don't touch him," the coach warned the man, who was shouting whatever wild insults came to his mind. The coach tried to coax him to calm down, but the man, whose eyes were glassy, raved rabidly as his arms flailed about.

I had been watching from upside-down on the bars, but got down to help Rosie gather her seeds. She was on her knees, face streaked and nose running. I pinched up three seeds from the ground before I turned to stand by the brothers who were still taunting the man with Coke bottles they had pulled from the garbage. Suddenly the man broke down and as loudly as he had screamed names, he screamed that he was sorry, that he didn't know what he was doing. He gathered his daughter in his arms, repeating again and again that he was sorry. The coach ushered him to the gate while the brothers, two of them crying, yelled that they were going to get him.

"You are no one, mister. You think you can do this to us because we're little," one said with his Coke bottle still cocked and ready.

I wanted to run for them as they left for their car, to explain that it was a mistake; that we also fell from the swings and the bars and slide and got hurt. I wanted to show the man my chin that broke open on the merry-go-round, the half-moon of pink scar. But they hurried away, sweaty from the morning sun, the man's pants and shirt stained with dirt and the little girl's limp dress smudged from her fall, and in some ways looking like us.

I returned to Rosie who was still collecting her seeds, and feeling bad but not knowing what to do, I got to my knees and asked if she wanted to play. I touched her hair, then her small shoulders, and called her name. She looked up at me, her face still wet from crying, and said, "Go away, Blackie."

That summer my eyes became infected. My brother and I had had a contest to see how long we could stare into the table fan without looking away. I was there for an hour, my head propped up in my hands, pretending all along I was in a biplane and the earth far below was World War I France. (That summer we watched *Dialing-for-Dollars*, a morning program that featured many war movies. Together we sat in a rocker-turned-fighter plane and machine-gunned everyone to death, both the good and the bad.)

An hour in front of the fan, and the next morning I woke with my eyes caked with mucus and unable to open them. I screamed to my mother who was in the kitchen stirring oatmeal, and when she came to the bedroom she screamed louder than me and fainted, dropping to the floor like a bundle of laundry. My brother rushed into the room with my sister following behind him, and both of them screamed when they saw Mom moaning on the ground. Looking up, they screamed as my hands searched the air, and flew to the living room. My mother woke with an *"Ay, Dios,"* bundled me in her arms, and carried me to the bathroom where she rinsed a hot wash cloth and rubbed it across my eyes, until the mucus softened and my lids fluttered open.

She screamed again because my eyes were not red but milky. She called the doctor who suggested an eye specialist, and that afternoon she took me to see the specialist with my eyes covered by a bandana. We were seen immediately. The nurse ushered us into a dimmed examining room where we were met by a doctor who lifted me into a chair whose motor whined until I was tilted far back. He pointed a small, chrome flashlight at each eye and with a Q-tip he tapped mucus from the corners of my eyes. With the lights back on, he squeezed eye drops between my spread lids, gave my mother instructions, and said it was important that I wear special sunglasses for the next three days. He fitted me with plastic smoke-colored glasses with paper earpieces.

"How's that, young man?" he said, trying to be cheerful. "You'll be just fine in a couple of days." He patted my knee and gave me a candy.

While Mother paid the receptionist I looked around the room, from the ceiling to the pictures of ships in a rough sea. It was smoky through the glasses. When we left the air-conditioned office the heat of the afternoon overwhelmed me, and I wanted to take off the glasses to wipe my nose of sweat, but Mother said that the light would make me go blind. We drove home in silence, past the smoky church and the smoky furniture store. I looked at my mother and she was smoky. Our block was smoky as we turned into it. My brother and sister, who greeted me with laughter, were darker than we'd left them. My mother scolded them and told them to water the lawn while we went inside where I was given a bowl of ice cream. I took this treat to the front window and looked out on a knot of smoky neighbor kids who were staring in silence. One of them asked if I was blind.

"No, Frostie," I called through the screened window. "I can still see your *mocos.*"

That night I was pampered by Mother; Rick and Debra grew envious because I was served more ice cream, more this and that, and was allowed to stay up until nine-thirty to watch *Dobie Gillis* in my smoky sunglasses. I could hear my brother in bed trying to talk to me.

"I'm going to get you, Gary," Rick said. I laughed especially loud at each funny scene, and when the program ended I said, "Boy, that was real good."

When I was sent to bed, I took off my sunglasses carefully and fogged them with my breath, rubbing them clean with my T-shirt. I placed them on the bureau and climbed into my bunk bed, while Rick muttered threats because he felt that I was being spoiled.

The next day we were again warned by our mother, who worked until four candling eggs for Safeway, not to go outside the house until one or the police might arrest her. The neighbors should not know that we were being left alone.

"But, Gary, you have to stay inside. I don't want you to go out in the sunlight." At the door she reminded me with a shake of her finger, "You heard what the doctor said. You can go blind, *m'ijo*."

I watched the morning movie in which John Wayne, injured in an attack on an aircraft carrier, had lost the ability to walk, but later, through courage and fortitude, he pulled himself out of bed, walked a few stiff steps, and collapsed just as the doctor and his girlfriend entered the room to witness his miracle comeback. I saw myself as John Wayne. Nearly blinded by a mean brother, I overcame my illness to become a fighter pilot who saves the world from the Japanese. I took a few Frankenstein steps across the living room, shouting that I was healed by the Lord. My brother countered with "You're not funny." He got up and went to the garage with Debra where they hammered on boards they said were going to be a scooter.

At one o'clock Rick and Debra went outside to ride their bikes in front of the house as I sat at the window yearning to join them. They rode by slowly, then with great speed, as they made certain to turn to me and smile to show they were really getting a kick out of riding their bikes. They rode for a while, their brows sweaty and their cheeks reddening, before an ice cream truck jingled up the block. They pulled together from their pockets seven cents for a juice bar which they took turns licking slowly under a tree. Rick looked at the window where I sat with my sunglasses on, and, very exaggeratedly, called out, "Ummm, good!"

They came inside, cooled off with Kool-Aid, and watched a game show neither of them cared for. Bored, Debra turned off the TV and went to her room to play with her dolls while Rick disappeared into the garage, where the rap of the hammer started up again. I peeked out the kitchen door that led to the garage, but he warned me that if I came out he would tell Mom.

Minutes later he came back into the living room where I was drawing and asked if I wanted to go to the playground.

"But Mom will get mad," I said.

"Ah, don't worry," he argued. "We'll be back before four. She won't know."

Debra returned to the living room and stood by Rick. Reluctant at first, I gave in when I saw them walk down the street without looking back, and trotted after them while holding onto my sunglasses so they wouldn't fall off.

At the playground I was a celebrity; the kids milled around me and asked if I was blind, did it hurt, would I have to wear the sunglasses forever? I played checkers and Candyland with Ronnie, happy that I was noticed by so many. Even the coach asked how I was, touched my hair and tenderly called me "knucklehead." This made Rick mad and when he said it was time to go home I told him it was only three-thirty and that Mom wouldn't get home until after four. Upset, he left with Debra tagging along in his shadow, but turned around before he was out of sight and said that he was going to get me. I played with Ronnie and sucked on a juice bar the coach had bought me, but left in a scramble when I discovered it was close to four.

As I returned home, happy as a pup, Rick jumped out from under a neighbor's hedge. "Now you're gonna get it, punk." His grin was mean and his eyes were narrowed like the Japanese I had seen on television that morning. Wrestling me to the ground, he scratched off my sunglasses, laughed a fake laugh, and ran away wearing them. Crying, and with my hands shading my brow, I rolled under the hedge Rick had jumped from because it was dark in there. The earth was cool and leaves stuck to my hair and T-shirt. I sat up Indian-style, squinting and calling for help, although no one came.

I tried to move but a branch stabbed my back and ripped

through my shirt, so I sat under the hedge calling out now and then, thinking that it was only a matter of time before I would go blind. An old woman with a shopping cart passed, and I called to her that I was going blind. She stopped, looked inside the hedge, her glasses slipping down from the bridge of her nose, and said, "Dear, I know just how you feel. Sometimes when I wake up in the morning, I can hardly make out where things are without my glasses." She turned away and continued down the street.

I started crying because I knew that when Mother discovered me under the hedge she would be mad. There would be no excuses. She would drag me home for a spanking while the neighbor kids watched.

Finally, about an hour later, I heard my mother's voice calling my name. I heard the clip-clop of my mother's sandals, her stern voice: "Where are you, *Chango*?"

"In the hedge, Mamma."

She bent down with her hands on her knees and squinted into the greenery. I squinted back and begged her not to hit me. Squatting, she waddled into the hedge, grabbed my wrist roughly, and tugged until I was standing up with my hands over my eyes. She fixed the sunglasses on my face and asked me what the hell I was doing in there.

"I didn't want to go blind. Rick took my sunglasses. They made me go to the playground," I whimpered incoherently, spilling it all. Once home, Rick got a spanking and Mom was raising a belt to punish me when I pointed to my sunglasses and cried out that I might really go blind. She stopped, her lips pursed, and just wagged her finger at me and warned that I would get a double dose the next time I misbehaved.

From the bedroom I could hear Rick whimpering into his pillow, "You're gonna get it, punk!"

One day the woman coach at the playground announced a crafts contest. The word went out in the morning when the kids gathered around her to hear what she had to say. Two kids sat in her lap while another played with her blonde curls as she broke the contest into categories: Drawing, lanyard, clay, and macaroni. First place winners would receive baseball caps. We oohed and aahed. The second and third place winners would get certificates. We oohed and aahed again.

"Now, kids, it's important to be original," she said. Someone asked what "original" meant.

"You know, different...You know, unique," she answered, and emphasized the definition with her hands.

I thought about this, and the next day for crafts period I came to the playground with a Frostie root beer bottle. At the picnic table under the tree I spray-painted it gold, let it dry in the sun, and after smearing it with glue rolled it into a pie tin of peat moss which shimmered a mystical gold. Pleased thus far, I then glued macaroni noodles that I had painted red to the neck of the bottle.

I worked in deep concentration as did the other kids, and when I finished I carried it very carefully to the game room where the coach sat on a stool behind a Dutch door thumbing through magazines. I looked up at her, smiling my happiness. She squinted and furrowed her brow when she saw my creation. "Ummm, interesting, Gary." She took it and placed it on a shelf.

The next day I made an ashtray. I rolled clay into a ball, pressed it out into a circle, and then raised the edges with a spoon. I made four dents where the cigarettes would rest, sticking colored buttons on each side of the dents.

That afternoon I also attempted a lanyard, but my patience with "loop and tuck, loop and tuck" gave out and I threw it into the garbage can. "Damn thing," I said under my breath as I walked to the game room to check out a four-square ball. I bounced it inordinately high in hopes of attracting the kids who were still working at their crafts under the tree. Few looked up and none left to join me; their dirty legs dangled motionless under the table.

At dinner that evening my sister and I described to our mother the excitement of the contest, each sure the other was out of the running.

"You should see my Frostie bottle, " I said to her as I ripped a tortilla and chewed loudly. "It's beautiful—like gold."

Debra described the toilet roll she had painted red and black with macaroni glued in a spiral like a barber's pole.

"Mine's the best, Mom!" Debra tore off a piece of tortilla and chewed louder than me, with her mouth open.

"Mom, I can see Debbie's food," I pointed with a fork. Debra chewed even louder, mocking me with her eyes spread wide like a bug's.

"OK, you kids, behave yourselves." Mom cleared the table as we scooted outside to play.

The next day I made a drawing of a dragster on fire. I outlined the lean body carefully, deliberating on each feature from the spoked wheels to the roll bar, and then scribbled the flames a vicious red and black, all the while whining like a car turning a corner. Finished, I carried it stiffly, as if I were in a pageant, to the game room. I handed it proudly to the coach who asked what it was.

"A dragster. That's the engine." I pointed out the eighteen pipes that hung on the side. I showed her the driver who had been thrown from the car. He was dead.

That afternoon the coach announced a special contest in which we could do anything we pleased.

"But it must be a secret," she said. All of the kids huddled in the shade because of the afternoon heat that rose above a hundred degrees. We listened quietly as she explained that we had to do it at home with our own materials and that we should be original. And again we asked what "original" meant, and again she explained, "You know, different... You know, unique," with her hands flashing out for definition.

Starry-eyed, my mind blazing with a seven-year-old's idea of beauty, I ran home because I knew exactly what I intended to produce. From the garbage I pulled a Campbell's soup can, ripped off the paper label, and in the garage painted it red with a stiff brush, the stifling heat wringing sweat from my face. I let the soup can dry in the sun, and that evening I glued rows of bottle caps that I had dug out with a spoon from a Coke machine: One row of Coca-Cola caps, then a row of Orange Crush, then one of Dr. Pepper, and so on. When I finished with this detail I packed dirt into the can, poked two pinto beans into it, and watered them carefully so the bottle caps wouldn't get wet and fall off.

I was pleased with my craft. When my mother came home that afternoon I took her by the hand to the back yard to show her.

"Very pretty." Her face was plain and unmoved, tired from a day's work of candling eggs, but still I grinned like a cat, already imagining that on Monday when the judging took place I was sure to win.

It was Friday when I finished the "special" craft, and I assumed that the next day the sprout of a pinto bean would break through the moist dirt. Nothing was there in the center of the can, so I watered it again with great care, every few hours checking to see if the beans had sprouted. Nothing.

Sunday arrived with still no sprout of greenery. Only two ants salvaging a feathery seed. I blew them from their task and again watered the beans, after which I placed the can on the fence rail in full sun and skipped off to play for the day, believing that when I returned home I would find the pale head of a bean plant pushing up from the dirt. I took the can off the fence. Nothing.

I brought the can into the garage where I pasted back the bottle caps that had fallen off from the sun's heat. I tapped the dirt, and it was hard. I again watered the seeds, praying they would grow.

"Come on, plants, get up. Tomorrow it's Monday."

Monday morning the plants had not come through, and although I was disappointed I still wanted to enter the can in the contest. With Debra, who had made a pencil holder from a toilet roll encircled with popsicle sticks, I went to the playground where I handed over my craft piece to the woman coach. That afternoon there was no crafts period; instead the man coach, along with a lady we didn't know, came to judge.

"How can you kids stand the heat?" the lady asked as she stepped into the game room fanning herself with a paper plate. She wore a white dress with a shiny red belt and a red hat, and looked very clean with her made-up face.

All the kids gathered around the Dutch door to try to hear what they were mumbling as they hovered over the crafts.

Caveman, an Okie kid whose closely cropped hair sloped at a forty-five degree angle, climbed the Dutch door, and before the woman coach could stop him he went up to the lady and tugged at her dress. Looking up to her with a face covered with snots, he asked her for a nickel. "I'm hungry."

Embarrassed, the woman coach apologized and scolded Caveman as she carried him from the game room. She told the rest of us to go and sit under the tree. Caveman ran off as a brother of Rosie's trailed him with his fists closed.

Finally, about half an hour later, the coaches, along with the well-dressed lady, came out and announced the names of the winners. Among them were Ronnie, Rosie, Weasel, Raymond, and even Caveman. They repeated the names because two prizes had been left out. That time around I had won third prize for my Frostie bottle! I screamed loudly, and screamed again when I saw the man coach lugging a bucket of iced Cokes that gleamed like fish. The woman coach arrived with popcorn and cookies, and we all screamed and laughed and argued throughout the afternoon.

When the party was over, my sister and I left with the crafts that hadn't won first place. Debra had won two second place certificates, and bragged all the way home and into autumn. Still, I was happy and taped my third place certificate to the bedroom wall. That evening after dinner I took my can to the front yard where I sat on the lawn sucking a blade of grass and wondered why the plants had not come up. My brother Rick rode by on his bike and yelled, "I told you I'd get you." I looked up at him as he rode off, and then looked at the can with realization. I scratched the surface of the dirt lightly and then dug with the full force of my finger nails. Nothing.

I looked up from the can and, with moist eyes, muttered, "My brother has to die."

Looking for Work

One July, while killing ants on the kitchen sink with a rolled newspaper, I had a nine-year-old's vision of wealth that would save us from ourselves. For weeks I had drunk Kool-Aid and watched morning reruns of *Father Knows Best*, whose family was so uncomplicated in its routine that I very much wanted to imitate it. The first step was to get my brother and sister to wear shoes at dinner.

"Come on, Rick—come on, Deb," I whined. But Rick mimicked me and the same day that I asked him to wear shoes he came to the dinner table in only his swim trunks. My mother didn't notice, nor did my sister, as we sat to eat our beans and tortillas in the stifling heat of our kitchen. We all gleamed like cellophane, wiping the sweat from our brows with the backs of our hands as we talked about the day: Frankie our neighbor was beat up by Faustino; the swimming pool at the playground would be closed for a day because the pump was broken.

Such was our life. So that morning, while doing-in the train of ants which arrived each day, I decided to become wealthy, and right away! After downing a bowl of cereal, I took a rake from the garage and started up the block to look for work.

We lived on an ordinary block of mostly working class people: warehousemen, egg candlers, welders, mechanics, and a union plumber. And there were many retired people who kept their lawns green and the gutters uncluttered of the chewing gum wrappers we dropped as we rode by on our bikes. They bent down to gather our litter, muttering at our evilness.

At the corner house I rapped the screen door and a very large woman in a muu-muu answered. She sized me up and then asked what I could do.

"Rake leaves," I answered, smiling.

"It's summer, and there ain't no leaves," she countered. Her face was pinched with lines; fat jiggled under her chin. She pointed to the lawn, then the flower bed, and said: "You see any leaves there—or there?" I followed her pointing arm, stupidly. But she had a job for me and that was to get her a Coke at the liquor store. She gave me twenty cents, and after ditching my rake in a bush, off I ran. I returned with an unbagged Pepsi, for which she thanked me and gave me a nickel from her apron.

I skipped off her porch, fetched my rake, and crossed the street to the next block where Mrs. Moore, mother of Earl the retarded man, let me weed a flower bed. She handed me a trowel and for a good part of the morning my fingers dipped into the moist dirt, ripping up runners of Bermuda grass. Worms surfaced in my search for deep roots, and I cut them in halves, tossing them to Mrs. Moore's cat who pawed them playfully as they dried in the sun. I made out Earl whose face was pressed to the back window of the house, and although he was calling to me I couldn't understand what he was trying to say. Embarrassed, I worked without looking up, but I imagined his contorted mouth and the ring of keys attached to his belt—keys that jingled with each palsied step. He scared me and I worked quickly to finish the flower bed. When I did finish Mrs. Moore gave me a quarter and two peaches from her tree, which I washed there but ate in the alley behind my house.

I was sucking on the second one, a bit of juice staining the front of my T-shirt, when Little John, my best friend, came walking down the alley with a baseball bat over his shoulder, knocking over trash cans as he made his way toward me.

Little John and I went to St. John's Catholic School, where we sat among the "stupids." Miss Marino, our teacher, alternated the rows of good students with the bad, hoping that by sitting side-by-side with the bright students the stupids might become more intelligent, as though intelligence were contagious. But we didn't progress as she had hoped. She grew frustrated when one day, while dismissing class for recess, Little John couldn't get up because his arms were stuck in the slats of the chair's backrest. She scolded us with a shaking finger when we knocked over the globe, denting the already troubled Africa. She muttered curses when Leroy White, a real stupid but a great softball player with the gift to hit to all fields, openly chewed his host when he made his First Communion; his hands swung at his sides as he returned to the pew looking around with a big smile.

Little John asked what I was doing, and I told him that I was taking a break from work, as I sat comfortably among high weeds. He wanted to join me, but I reminded him that the last time he'd gone door-to-door asking for work his mother had whipped him. I was with him when his mother, a New Jersey Italian who could rise up in anger one moment and love the next, told me in a polite but matter-of-fact voice that I had to leave because she was going to beat her son. She gave me a homemade popsicle, ushered me to the door, and said that I could see Little John the next day. But it was sooner than that. I went around to his bedroom window to suck my popsicle and watch Little John dodge his mother's blows, a few hitting their mark but many whirring air.

It was midday when Little John and I converged in the alley, the sun blazing in the high nineties, and he suggested that we go to Roosevelt High School to swim. He needed five cents to make fifteen, the cost of admission, and I lent him a nickel. We ran home for my bike and when my sister found out that we were going swimming, she started to cry because she didn't have the fifteen cents but only an empty Coke bottle. I waved for her to come and three of us mounted the bike—Debra on the cross bar, Little John on the handle bars and holding the Coke bottle which we would cash for a nickel and make up the difference that would allow all of us to get in, and me pumping up the crooked streets, dodging cars and pot holes. We spent the day swimming under the afternoon sun, so that when we got home our mom asked us what was darker, the floor or us? She feigned a stern posture, her hands on her hips and her mouth puckered. We played along. Looking down, Debbie and I said in unison, "Us."

That evening at dinner we all sat down in our bathing suits to eat our beans, laughing and chewing loudly. Our mom was in a good mood, so I took a risk and asked her if sometime we could have turtle soup. A few days before I had watched a television program in which a Polynesian tribe killed a large turtle, gutted it, and then stewed it over an open fire. The turtle, basted in a sugary sauce, looked delicious as I ate an afternoon bowl of cereal, but my sister, who was watching the program with a glass of Kool-Aid between her knees, said, "Caca."

My mother looked at me in bewilderment. "Boy, are you a crazy Mexican. Where did you get the idea that people eat turtles?"

"On television," I said, explaining the program. Then I took it a step further. "Mom, do you think we could get dressed up for dinner one of these days? David King does."

"*Ay, Dios,*" my mother laughed. She started collecting the dinner plates, but my brother wouldn't let go of his. He was still drawing a picture in the bean sauce. Giggling, he said it was me, but I didn't want to listen because I wanted an answer from Mom. This was the summer when I spent the mornings in front of the television that showed the comfortable lives of white kids. There were no beatings, no rifts in the family. They wore bright clothes; toys tumbled from their closets. They hopped into bed with kisses and woke to glasses of fresh orange juice, and to a father sitting before his morning coffee while the mother buttered his toast. They hurried through the day making friends and gobs of money, returning home to a warmly lit living room, and then dinner. *Leave It To Beaver* was the program I replayed in my mind:

"May I have the mashed potatoes?" asks Beaver with a smile.

"Sure, Beav," replies Wally as he taps the corners of his mouth with a starched napkin.

The father looks on in his suit. The mother, decked out in earrings and a pearl necklace, cuts into her steak and blushes. Their conversation is politely clipped.

"Swell," says Beaver, his cheeks puffed with food.

Our own talk at dinner was loud with belly laughs and marked by our pointing forks at one another. The subjects were commonplace.

"Gary, let's go to the ditch tomorrow," my brother suggests. He explains that he has made a life preserver out of four empty detergent bottles strung together with twine and that he will make me one if I can find more bottles. "No way are we going to drown."

"Yeah, then we could have a dirt clod fight," I reply, so happy to be alive.

Whereas the Beaver's family enjoyed dessert in dishes at the table, our mom sent us outside, and more often than not I went into the alley to peek over the neighbor's fences and spy out fruit, apricot or peaches.

I had asked my mom and again she laughed that I was a crazy *chavalo* as she stood in front of the sink, her arms rising and falling with suds, face glistening from the heat. She sent me outside where my brother and sister were sitting in the shade that the fence threw out like a blanket. They were talking about me when I plopped down next to them. They looked at one another and then Debbie, my eight-year-old sister, started in.

"What's this crap about getting dressed up?"

She had entered her profanity stage. A year later she would give up such words and slip into her Catholic uniform, and into squealing on my brother and me when we "cussed this" and "cussed that."

I tried to convince them that if we improved the way we looked we might get along better in life. White people would like us more. They might invite us to places, like their homes or front yards. They might not hate us so much.

My sister called me a "craphead," and got up to leave with a stalk of grass dangling from her mouth. "They'll never like us."

My brother's mood lightened as he talked about the ditch—the white water, the broken pieces of glass, and the rusted car fenders that awaited our knees. There would be toads, and rocks to smash them.

David King, the only person we knew who resembled the middle class, called from over the fence. David was Catholic, of Armenian and French descent, and his closet was filled with toys. A bear-shaped cookie jar, like the ones on television, sat on the kitchen counter. His mother was remarkably kind while she put up with the racket we made on the street. Evenings, she often watered the front yard and it must have upset her to see us—my brother and I and others—jump from trees laughing, the unkillable kids of the very poor, who got up unshaken, brushed off, and climbed into another one to try again.

David called again. Rick got up and slapped grass from his pants. When I asked if I could come along he said no. David said no. They were two years older so their affairs were different from mine. They greeted one another with foul names and took off down the alley to look for trouble.

I went inside the house, turned on the television, and was about to sit down with a glass of Kool-Aid when Mom shooed me outside.

"It's still light," she said. "Later you'll bug me to let you stay out longer. So go on."

I downed my Kool-Aid and went outside to the front yard. No one was around. The day had cooled and a breeze rustled the trees. Mr. Jackson, the plumber, was watering his lawn and when he saw me he turned away to wash off his front steps. There was more than an hour of light left, so I took advantage of it and decided to look for work. I felt suddenly alive as I skipped down the block in search of an overgrown flower bed and the dime that would end the day right.

Deceit

For four years I attended St. John's Catholic School where short nuns threw chalk at me, chased me with books cocked over their heads, squeezed me into cloak closets and, on slow days, asked me to pop erasers and to wipe the blackboard clean. Finally, in the fifth grade, my mother sent me to Jefferson Elementary. The Principal, Mr. Buckalew, kindly ushered me to the fifth grade teachers, Mr. Stendhal and Mrs. Sloan. We stood in the hallway with the principal's hand on my shoulder. Mr. Stendhal asked what book I had read in the fourth grade, to which, after a dark and squinting deliberation, I answered: *The Story of the United States Marines*. Mr. Stendhal and Mrs. Sloan looked at one another with a "you take him" look. Mr. Buckalew lifted his hand from my shoulder and walked slowly away.

Mrs. Sloan took me into her classroom where, perhaps, the most memorable thing she said to us all year was that she loved to chew tar.

Our faces went sour. "What kind of tar?"

"Oh, street tar—it's like gum." Her hands were pressed into a chapel as she stared vacantly over our heads in some yearning for the past.

And it was an odd year for me because there were months on end when I was the sweet kid who wanted to become a priest. In turn, there were the months when I was your basic kid with a rock in his hand.

When the relatives came over to talk to me and pat me on the head, they often smiled and asked what I wanted to be when I grew up.

"A priest," I would say during those docile months, while if they caught me during the tough months I would answer, "A hobo, I think."

They would smile and chuckle, "Oh, Gary."

Although I was going to public school, my brother, sister, and I were still expected to go to church. We would dress in our best clothes, with Debra in a yellow bonnet that she would throw into a bush just around the corner. "Stupid thing," she muttered as she hid it under the leaves with the intention of getting it later.

After a month or so Rick and Debra didn't have to go to church; instead they lounged in their pajamas drinking hot chocolate and talking loudly of how they were going to spend the morning watching television. I was, as my mom described me, a "short-tail devil in need of God's blessings."

So each Sunday I put on a white shirt and stepped into a pair of pants that kicked around my ankles, my white socks glowing on my feet in the dark pews of St. John's Cathedral. I knelt, I rose, and I looked around. I muddled prayers and knocked my heart with a closed hand when the priest knelt and the altar boy followed with a jingle of the bell.

For the first few weeks I went to church, however reluctantly, but soon discovered the magazine rack at Mayfair Market, which was only two blocks from the church. I read comics and chewed gum, with only a sliver of guilt about missing Mass pricking my soul. When I returned home after the hour that it took to say a Mass, my mom was in the kitchen but didn't ask about the Mass—what the priest said or did I drop the quarter she had given me into the donation basket. Instead, she handed me a buttered tortilla as a reward for being a good boy, and I took it to eat in my bedroom. I chuckled under my breath, "God, this is great."

The next week at the magazine rack I read about Superman coming back to life, chewed gum, and took swigs of a Coke I had bought with money intended for the far-reaching wicker basket. But the following week I came up with another idea: I started happily up the street while my mom looked out the front window with hands on hips, but once around the corner I swung into the alley to see what I could do.

That Sunday I played with Little John, and the following

week I looked through a box of old magazines before dismantling a discarded radio. I gutted it of its rusty tubes and threw them, one by one, at a fence until a neighbor came out and told me to get the hell away.

Another Sunday I went up the street into the alley and climbed the fence of our back yard. Our yard was sectioned into two by a fence: The front part was neatly mowed, colored with flowers and cemented with a patio, while the back part was green with a vegetable garden, brown with a rusty incinerator, and heaped with odd junk—ruined bicycles, boards, buckled wheel-barrows. I climbed into the back part of our long yard and pressed my face between the slats: Rick was hoeing a flower bed while Debra was waiting to clean up with a box in her hands. My mom was washing down the patio.

I laughed to myself and then made a cat sound. When no one looked up, I meowed again and Mom looked in my direction for a second, then lowered her eyes to the water bouncing off the patio. I again laughed to myself, but quieted when Rick opened the gate to dump a load of weeds into the compost. I was smiling my evilness behind an old dismantled gate, and when he left I meowed again, chuckled to myself, and climbed the fence into the alley to look around for something to do.

This would continue all through the summer of my twelfth year, and by fall Mom said I didn't have to go to church because she had seen an improvement in my ways.

"See, I told you, *m'ijo*," she said over dinner one night. "The nuns would be very proud of you."

I swallowed a mouthful of beans and cleared my throat. "Yes, Mom."

Still, when relatives showed up at the door to talk to my mom in Spanish, I hung around to comb my hair and wait for them to open their purses or fiddle deeply in their pockets for a nickel or dime. They would pat my head and ask me what I wanted to be when I grew up. "A priest," I would answer, to which they would smile warmly, "Oh, Gary," and give over the coin.

Catholics

I was standing in the waste basket for fighting on the day we received a hunger flag for Biafra. Sister Marie, a tough nun who could throw a softball farther than most men, read a letter that spoke of the grief of that country, looking up now and then to measure our sympathy and to adjust her glasses that had slipped from her nose. She read the three-page letter, placed it on her desk, and walked over to the globe to point out Africa, a continent of constant dispair. I craned my neck until, without realizing it, I had one foot out of the wastebasket. Sister Marie turned and stared me back into place, before she went on to lecture us about hunger.

"Hunger is a terrible, terrible thing," she began. "It robs the body of its vitality and the mind of its glory, which is God's."

Sister Marie cruised slowly up and down the rows, tapping a pencil in her palm and talking about death, hunger, and the blessed infants, which were God's, until the students hung their heads in fear or boredom. Then she brightened up.

"With hunger, heavier people would live longer—they have more fat, you see." She tapped her pencil, looked around the room, and pointed to Gloria Leal. "If we didn't have any food whatsoever, Gloria would probably live the longest." Hands folded neatly on her desk, Gloria forced a smile but didn't look around the room at the students who had turned to size her up.

Sister Marie walked up another row, still tapping her pencil and talking about hunger, when she pointed to me. "And Gary...well, he would be one of the first to die." Students turned in their chairs to look at me with their mouths open, and I was mad, not for being pointed out but because of that unfair lie. I could outlive the whole class, food or no food. Wasn't I one of the meanest kids in the entire school? Didn't I beat up Chuy Hernandez, a bigger kid? I shook my head in disbelief, and said "nah" under my breath.

Sister Marie glared at me, almost bitterly, as she told the class again that I would be the first one to die. She tapped her pencil as she walked slowly up to me. Scared, I looked away, first up to the ceiling and then to a fly that was walking around on the floor. But my head was snapped up when Sister Marie pushed my chin with her pencil. She puckered her mouth into a clot of lines and something vicious raged in her eyes, like she was getting ready to throw a softball. What it was I didn't know, but I feared that she was going to squeeze me from the waste basket and hurl me around the room. After a minute or so her face relaxed and she returned to the front of the class where she announced that for the coming three weeks we would collect money daily for Biafra.

"The pagan babies depend on our charitable hearts," she said. She looked around the room and returned to the globe where she again pointed out Africa. I craned my head and pleaded, "Let me see." She stared me back into place and then resumed talking about the fruits of the world, some of which were ours and some of which were not ours.

The Beauty Contest

It had been a sticky and difficult week of two nose bleeds from bigger kids when Karen, the coach at Romain playground, announced that there was going to be a children's beauty contest. I was in the elm tree above the picnic table where we played Old Maid and Sorry. Two kids were bent over a game, and I was bombing them with small pieces of bark, thinking all along that their shaved or tangled heads were World War II Germany. They laughed when the bark landed quietly as flies, and shook them from their hair so I would do it again.

I asked the coach what a "beauty contest" was, and she answered that it was like a game to see who was the best looking. "But you're too old, Blackie," she told me. "It's for little kids." Since I was nine I dismissed it from my mind and went on dropping bombs, but later, when I returned home to smack together a peanut butter and jelly sandwich, I thought of my smaller brother, Jimmy. A tough kid, he was jumping up and down on the couch with a sandwich in his hand—a chipped front tooth showing gray when he was ready to bite. As I worked on my second sandwich I thought more and more about entering Jimmy. Strong build, a chipped tooth, half Mexican and half white—he might win, I thought.

Jimmy was not yet four, so when I told him about what I wanted him to do, he said OK. I ran to his drawer and searched for a bathing suit—an orange thing with an anchor in the front and a paint stain on the back. Undressed, he tugged his way into it and that afternoon he practiced walking.

"Leave your hands at your side," I instructed him as he

marched from the kitchen to the living room. "Look left and then right, like you're going to cross the street. Yeah, that's good—and smile like you're going to eat some chicken. They want to see that tooth."

I combed his hair and shined his face with Jergen's lotion and made him walk until he got it right. After that we turned on the television and waited for the week to pass.

On the day of the event I dressed Jimmy in his bathing suit with a clean T-shirt and lent him my rubber thongs. They were too big, like snowshoes, but I thought them more appropriate than his high top tennies. I slipped into hemmed cut-offs, a white shirt, and shoes that gleamed black as roaches. I smeared his face with Jergen's lotion and combed his waxed hair until it followed a stiff but clean grain. As we walked through the street a few neighbor kids were playing a game of "pickle"; they stopped for a few seconds to ask where we were going. Why were we so dressed up? They looked at us in awe, and I felt important at telling them that we were off to a "beauty contest."

We got to the playground just as mothers arrived in station wagons—mothers in bubble-shaped sunglasses, straw hats with different fruits on the brims, and sharkskin skirts. Cameras dangled from their wrists; purses were pressed under their armpits. Some banged aluminum folding chairs from car trunks and set them before the swimming pool where the contest would be held. Jimmy and I looked happily at the balloons that tossed softly on the gate and the strings of plastic flags—those familiar ones from used car lots—drooped on the fence.

Jimmy and I sat under the elm with Rosie, Raymond, Caveman and a few others, and although none of us said anything we were awed by the blond and fair-skinned kids in good clothes. They looked beautiful, I thought, with their cheeks flushed red from the morning heat. The kids stood close to their mothers and wore fancy shirts, sundresses with prints of zoos or bright balloons, and tiny hats—sailor, farm boy, or grassy things with plastic animals holding hands.

With a bullhorn the coach called for the girls to line up. Mothers bent to give hugs and whisper last-minute instructions to their daughters before they were pushed gently through the gate where the coach smiled, pinned numbers on the backs of their suits, and lined them up by height. When they were called out to walk around the pool, some of them looked scared as they searched for their mothers, who clung to the fence or took pictures; other girls looked down at their feet, with fingers in their mouths. They paraded around the pool until they had been sized up by the three women judges who scratched notes behind card tables. The girls were then asked to sit down on the lawn that outlined the pool as the boys were called through the bullhorn to make a line at the gate.

Jimmy and I ran to the gate. I reminded him what to do and, somewhat scared by it all, he nodded his head "yes" and tugged at his bathing suit. The coach called for the line to march in, and it moved slowly into the pool area with most of the boys looking down at the blue of the water, not at their mothers.

Because he was the smallest, Jimmy went out first and did as I had instructed: He looked left, then right; he smiled like he was going to eat chicken, pulling back his lips to show his tooth. He walked stiffly before the judges and took his place behind the tallest boy.

I clung to the fence, with Rosie and Caveman at my side, as one after another the boys marched around the pool and past the judges who tapped their pencils and looked at one another before they scratched notes. Rosie touched my arm when one of the boys, just before he was called, put on a pair of sunglasses with pistols at the corners. As he started, I heard laughter from the elm tree and the words: "Sissy boy."

When all the boys had circled the pool, they, too, were asked to sit on the lawn with the girls who were reddening like crabs from the warm weather. The judges craned their heads together, whispered seriously, and then whispered again.

With the bullhorn the coach asked for the boys and girls to join hands and parade around the pool. They looked at one another, unsure of what she was saying. The coach talked with the bullhorn again, but still they were confused at what to do. One kid stepped up to the edge of the pool and, looking up at the coach, asked: "Do you want us to jump in?"

The coach climbed down from her station, smiling and shaking her head as she passed the parents to go over to explain to the kids what they were supposed to do. Finally, hand in hand, they paraded awkwardly—the boys looking at the water and the girls waving at their mothers.

The judges converged behind the children who once again had lined up by height. One judge took control and waved a paper crown of glitter over the girls while the parents clung even harder to the fence. When the crown dropped softly on a little girl with curlicues, moans were let out. One mother squeaked, clapped her hands like a loud rain, and looked around for someone to share her excitement. The other mothers looked away and tapped the cameras in their palms. When another crown dropped on a boy's head, there were more moans. Another mother smiled but contained her happiness as the boy was given a trophy and tickets to see the Fresno Giants. Raymond, who was lost in the green leaves of the elm, called down at the winner: "You're a sissy." A mother searched the tree, with a sour and disgusted look, but couldn't spot his brown legs.

I was disappointed. Rosie and Caveman ran away to play on the swings without saying anything as I stepped away from the fence and sat under the elm. Raymond dropped a piece of bark on my head and made the sound of a bomb exploding. Without looking up, I told him to leave me alone, and he did. The tree shook as he moved to a higher limb.

The Prince and Princess again went around the pool while a reporter from the *Fresno Bee* on one knee took pictures. At the ceremony's end, the gate was swung open and the losers were handed ice cream sandwiches as they left to join the onlookers. The coach spoke through the bullhorn, thanking everyone for coming. From a top branch Raymond called his own thanks through cupped hands: "See you later, alligator; after awhile, crocodile." He laughed at his joke and the tree shook again as he moved to another branch. The coach, Karen, walked over and, shading her eyes, squinted into the branches. Raymond dropped a piece of bark on her and made the sound of a bomb exploding.

"Raymond, is that you?" she shouted. "Raymond, is that you?" he mimicked. "Get down here right this minute," she warned. "Get down here right this minute," a branch said. More bombs fell, followed by explosions.

Karen shook her head at the mothers who were gathering chairs and lugging ice chests back to their station wagons. "These kids are so terrible." She shook her head, tsssked "Is he in trouble," and sent me to the game room for a football to knock Raymond from the tree.

Baseball in April

For three springs my brother and I walked to Romain playground
to try out for Little League, and year after year we failed to
impress the coaches. The night of the last year we tried out, we
sat in our bedroom listening to the radio and pounding our fists
into gloves, and talked of how we would bend to pick up
grounders, stand at the plate, wave off another player to say you
got the pop-up. "This is the year," Rick said with confidence as
he pretended to back hand a ball and throw out the man racing
to first. He pounded his glove and looked at me, "How'd you like
that?"

At the tryouts there were a hundred kids. After asking
around, we were pointed to lines by age group: nine, ten, and
eleven. Rick and I stood in our respective lines, gloves limp as
dead animals hanging from our hands, and waited to have a
large paper number pinned to our back so that field coaches with
clipboards propped on their stomachs would know who we were.

Nervous, I chewed at my palm as I moved up in the line, but
when my number was called I ran out onto the field to the sound
of my sneakers smacking against the clay. I looked at the kids
still in line, then at my brother who was nodding his head yes.
The first grounder—a three-bouncer that spun off my glove into
center field. Another grounder cracked off the bat, and I bent
down to gobble it up: The ball fell from my glove like food from
a sloppy mouth. I stared at the ball before I picked it up to hurl it
to first base. The next one I managed to pick up cleanly, but my
throw made the first baseman leap into the air with an
exaggerated grunt that had him looking good while I looked bad.

Three more balls were hit to me, and I came up with one.

So it went for me, my number flapping like a single, broken wing as I ran off the field to sit in the bleachers and wait for Rick to trot onto the field.

He was a star that day. With the first grounder he raced for it and threw on the run. With the next ball he lowered himself on one knee and threw nonchalantly to first. His number flapped on his back, a crooked seventeen, and I saw a coach make a check on his board. He then looked serious as he wet his lips and wrote something that demanded thought, for his brow furrowed and darkened.

Rick lunged at the next hit and missed it as it skidded into center field. With the next hit he shaded his eyes for it was a high pop-up, something that he was good at, even graceful, and when the ball fell earthward he slapped it with his toe and looked pleased as his mouth grew fat from trying to hold back a smile. Again the coach wet his lips and made a check on his clipboard.

Rick did well at fielding. When the next number was called, he jogged off the field with his head high and both of us sat in the bleachers, dark and serious as we watched the others trot on and off the field.

Finally the coaches told us to return after lunch to take batting practice. Rick and I ran home to fix sandwiches and talk about the morning, then what to expect in the afternoon.

"Don't be scared," he said with his mouth full of sandwich. He was thinking of my batting. He demonstrated how to stand. He spread his legs, worked his left foot into the carpet as if he were putting out a cigarette, and looked angrily at where the ball would be delivered, some twenty feet in front of him at the kitchen table. He swung an invisible bat; choked up and swung again.

He turned to me. "You got it?" I told him I thought I did and imitated his motion as I stepped where he was standing to swing once, then again and then again, until he said, "Yeah, you got it."

We returned to the playground, and I felt proud walking to the diamond because smaller kids were watching us in awe, some of them staring at the paper number on my back. It was as if we were soldiers going off to war.

"Where you goin'?"asked Rosie, sister of Johnnie Serna, the playground terrorist. She was squeezing the throat of a large bag of sunflower seeds, her mouth rolling with shells.

"Tryouts," I said, barely looking at her as I kept stride with Rick.

At the diamond I once again grew scared and apprehensive. I got into the line of nine-year-olds to wait for my turn at bat. Fathers clung to the fence, chattering last minute instructions to their kids who answered with, "OK, yes, all right, OK, OK," because they were also wide-eyed and scared when the kid in the batter's box swung and missed.

By the time it was my turn I was shivering unnoticeably and trying to catch Rick's eyes for reassurance. When my number was called I walked to the plate, tapped the bat on the ground—something I had seen many times on television—and waited. The first pitch was outside and over my head. The coach who was on the mound laughed at his sorry pitch.

At the next pitch I swung hard, spinning the ball foul. I tapped my bat again, kicked at the dirt, and stepped into the batter's box. I swung stupidly at a low ball; I wound up again and sliced the ball foul, just at the edge of the infield grass, which surprised me because I didn't know I had the strength to send it that far.

I was given ten pitches and managed to get three hits, all of them grounders on the right side. One of them kicked up into the face of a kid trying to field; he tried to hang tough as he walked off the field, head bowed and quiet, but I knew tears were welling up in his eyes.

I handed the bat to the next kid and went to sit in the bleachers to wait for the ten-year-olds to come up to bat. I was feeling better after that morning's tryout at fielding beause I had three hits. I also thought I looked good standing cocky at the plate, bat high over my shoulder.

Rick came up to the plate and hit the first pitch on the third base side. He sent the next pitch into left field. He talked to himself as he stood in the box, slightly bouncing before each swing. Again the coaches made checks on their clipboards, heads following the ball each time it was smacked to the outfield.

When the ten hits were up he jogged off the field and joined me in the bleachers. His mouth was again fat from holding back a smile, and I was jealous of his athletic display. I thought to myself, Yeah, he'll make the team and I'll just watch him from the bleachers. I felt bad—empty as a Coke bottle—as I imagined Rick running home with a uniform under his arm.

We watched other kids come to the plate and whack, foul, chop, slice, dribble, bee line, and hook balls to every part of the field. One high foul ball bounced in the bleachers and several kids raced to get it, but I was the first to latch a hand onto it. I weighed the ball in my palm, like a pound of baloney, and then hurled it back onto the field. A coach watched it roll by his feet, disinterested.

After tryouts were finished we were told—or retold, because it had been announced in the morning—that we would be contacted by phone late in the week.

We went home and by Monday afternoon we were already waiting for the phone to ring. We slouched in the living room after school, with the TV turned on and loud as a roomful of people: *Superman* at three o'clock and *The Three Stooges* at three-thirty. Every time I left the living room for the kitchen, I stole a glance at the telephone and once when no one was looking I picked it up to see if it was working: a long buzz.

By Friday when it was clear that the call would never come, we went outside to the front yard to play catch and practice bunting.

"I should have made the team," Rick said as he made a stab at my bunt. He was particularly troubled because if anyone should have made the team it was him, since he was better than most that day.

We threw grounders at one another; a few of them popped off my chest while most of them disappeared neatly into my glove. Why couldn't I do it like this last Saturday, I thought? I was mad at myself, then sad and self-pitying. We stopped playing and returned inside to watch *The Three Stooges*. Moe was reading from a children's story book, his finger following the words with deliberation.

"Does the doe have a deer?" read Moe.

"Yeah, two bucks," laughed Larry.

Moe pounded him on top of the head and called him a "knuckle-head." Larry rolled his eyes and looked dizzy.

We didn't make Little League that year, but we did join a team of school chums that practiced at Hobo Park near downtown

Fresno. Pete, the brother of Mary Palacio, a girl who was head-over-heels for me, told us about the team, and after school Rick and I raced our bicycles to the park. We threw our bikes aside and hit the field. While Rick went to the outfield, I took second base to practice grounders.

"Give me a baby roller,"Danny Lopez, the third baseman, called. I sidearmed a roller and he picked it up on the third bounce. "Good pickup," we told him. He looked pleased, slapping his glove against his pants as he hustled back to third, a smile cutting across his face.

Rick practiced pop-ups with Billy Reeves. They looked skyward with each throw in the air, mouths hanging open as if God were making a face between clouds.

When Manuel, the coach, arrived in his pickup, most of the kids ran to meet him and chatter that they wanted to play first, to play second, to hit first, to hit third. Rick and I went quiet and stood back from the racket.

Manuel shouldered a duffle bag from the back of his pickup and walked over to the palm tree that served as the backstop. He let the bag drop with a grunt, clapped his hands, and pointed kids to positions. We were still quiet, and when Pete told Manuel that we wanted to play, I stiffened up and tried to look tough. I popped my glove with my fist and looked about me as if I were readying to cross a road. Because he was older, Rick stood with his arms crossed over his chest, glove at his feet. "You guys in the outfield," he pointed as he turned to pull a bat and ball from the bag.

Manuel was middle-aged, patient, and fatherly. He bent down on his haunches to talk to kids. He spoke softly and showed interest in what we had to say. He cooed "good" when we made catches, even routine ones. We all knew he was good to us because most of the kids on the team didn't have fathers or, if they did, the fathers were so beaten from hard work that they never spent time with them. They came home to open the refrigerator for a beer and then to plop in front of the TV. They didn't even have the energy to laugh when something was funny. Rick and I saw this in our stepfather. While we might have opened up with laughter at a situation comedy, he just stared at the pictures flashing before him—unmoved, eyes straight ahead.

We practiced for two weeks before Manuel announced that he

had scheduled our first game.

"Who we playing?" someone asked.

"The Red Caps," he answered. "West Fresno boys."

By that time I had gotten better. Rick had quit the team because of a new girlfriend, a slow walker who hugged her school books against her chest while looking like a dazed boxer at Rick's equally dazed face. Stupid, I thought, and rode off to practice.

Although I was small I was made catcher. I winced behind my mask when the ball was delivered and the batter swung because there was no chest protector or chin guards—just a mask. Balls skidded off my arms and chest, but I didn't let on that they hurt—though once I doubled over after having the breath knocked out of me. Manuel hovered over me while rubbing my stomach and cooing words that made me feel better.

My batting, however, did not improve, and everyone on the team knew I was a "sure out." Some of the older kids tried to give me tips—how to stand, follow through, push weight into the ball.... Still, when I came up to bat, everyone moved in, like soldiers edging in for the attack. A slow roller to short, and I raced to first with my teeth showing. Out by three steps.

The day of the first game some of us met early at Hobo Park to talk about how we were going to whip them and send them home whining to their mothers. Soon others showed up to practice fielding grounders while waiting for the coach to pull up in his pickup. When we spotted him coming down the street, we ran to him and before the pickup had come to a stop we were already climbing the sides. The coach stuck his head from the cab to warn us to be careful. He idled the pickup for a few minutes to wait for the others, and when two did come running, he waved for them to get in the front with him. As he drove slowly to the West Side, our hair flicked about in the wind, and we thought we looked neat.

When we arrived we leaped from the back but stayed close by the coach who waved to the other coach as he pulled the duffle bag over his shoulder. He then scanned the other team: Like us, most were Mexican, although there were a few blacks. We had a few Anglos on our team—Okies, as we called them.

The coach shook hands with the other coach and talked quietly in Spanish, then opened up with laughter that had them patting one another's shoulder. Quieting, they turned around and considered the field, pointed to the outfield where the sprinkler heads jutted from the grass. They scanned the infield and furrowed their brows at where shortstop would stand: it was pitted from a recent rain. They parted talking in English and our coach returned to tell us the rules.

We warmed up behind the backstop, throwing softly to one another and trying to look calm. We spied the other team and they, in turn, spied us. They seemed bigger and darker, and wore matching T-shirts and caps. We were mismatched in jeans and T-shirts.

At bat first, we scored one run on an error and a double to left field. When the other team came up, they scored four runs on three errors. With the last one I stood in front of the plate, mask in hand, yelling for the ball.

"I got a play! I got a play!" The ball sailed over my head and hit the backstop, only to ricochet in foul ground on the first base side. The runner was already sitting on the bench, breathing hard and smiling, by the time I picked up the ball. I walked it to the pitcher.

I searched his face and he was scared. He was pressed to the wall and he was falling apart. I told him he could do it. "C'mon baby," I said, arm around his shoulder, and returned to behind the plate. I was wearing a chest protector that reached almost to my knees and made me feel important. I scanned the bleachers— a sad three-row display case—and Mary Palacio was talking loudly with a friend, indifferent to the game.

We got out of the first inning without any more runs. Then, at bat, we scored twice on a hit and an error that felled their catcher. He was doubled over his knees, head bowed like someone ready to commit hara-kiri, and rocking back and forth, smothering the small bursts of yowls. We went on to add runs, but so did they; by the eighth inning they were ahead, sixteen to nine.

As the innings progressed our team started to argue with one another. Our play was sloppy, nothing like the cool routines back at Hobo Park. Flyballs that lifted to the outfield dropped at the feet of open-mouthed players. Grounders rolled slowly between awkward feet. The pitching was sad.

"You had to mess up, *menso*," Danny Lopez screamed at the

shortstop.

"Well, you didn't get a hit, and *I* did," the shortstop said, pointing to his chest.

The coach clung to the screen as if he were hanging from a tall building and the earth was far below. He let us argue and only looked at us with a screwed up face when he felt we were getting out of hand.

I came up for the fourth time that day in the eighth with two men on. My teammates were grumbling because they thought I was going to strike out, pop-up, roll it back to the pitcher, anything but hit the ball. I was scared because the other team had changed pitchers and was throwing "fire," as we described it.

"Look at those 'fireballs'," the team whispered in awe from the bench as player after player swung through hard strikes, only to return to the dugout, head down and muttering. "What fire," we all agreed.

I came up scared of the fast ball and even more scared of failing. Mary looked on from the bleachers with a sandwich in her hands. The coach clung to the screen, cooing words. The team yelled at me to hit it hard. Dig in, they suggested, and I dug in, bat high over my shoulder as if I were really going to do something. And I did. With two balls and a strike, the pitcher threw "fire" that wavered toward my thigh. Instead of jumping out of the way I knew I had to let the ball hit me because that was the only way I was going to get on base. I grimaced just before it hit with a thud and grimaced even harder when I went down holding my leg and on the verge of crying. The coach ran from the dugout to hover over me on his haunches and rub my leg, coo words, and rub again. A few team members stood over me with their hands on their knees, with concerned faces but stupid questions: "Does it hurt?" "Can I play catcher now?" "Let me run for him, coach!"

But I rose and limped to first, the coach all along asking if I was OK. He shooed the team back into the dugout, then jogged to stand in the coach's box at first. Although my leg was pounding like someone at the door, I felt happy to be on first. I grinned, looked skyward, and adjusted my cap. "So this is what it's like," I thought to myself. I clapped my hands and encouraged the batter, our lead off man. "C'mon, baby, c'mon, you can do it." He hit a high fly ball to center, but while the staggering player lined up to pick it from the air, I rounded second on my way to third, feeling wonderful that I had gotten that far.

We lost nineteen to eleven and would go on to lose against the Red Caps four more times because they were the only team we would ever play. A two-team league. But that's what it was that spring.

The sad part is that I didn't know when the league ended. As school grew to a close, fewer and fewer of the players came to play, so that there were days when we were using girls to fill the gaps. Finally one day Manuel didn't show up with his duffle bag over his shoulder. On that day I think it was clear to us—the three or four who remained—that it was all over, though none of us let on to the others. We threw the ball around, played pickle, and then practiced pitching. When dusk began to settle, we lifted our bicycles and rode home. I didn't show up the next day for practice but instead sat in front of the television watching Superman bend iron bars.

I felt guilty, though, because I was thinking that one of the players might have arrived for practice only to find a few sparrows hopping about on the lawn. If he had he might have waited on the bench or, restless and embarrassed, he may have practiced pop-ups by throwing the ball into the air, calling "I got it," and trying it again all by himself.

Fear

A cold day after school. Frankie T., who would drown his brother by accident that coming spring and would use a length of pipe to beat a woman in a burglary years later, had me pinned on the ground behind a backstop, his breath sour as meat left out in the sun. *"Cabron,"* he called me and I didn't say anything. I stared at his face, shaped like the sole of a shoe, and just went along with the insults, although now and then I tried to raise a shoulder in a halfhearted struggle because that was part of the game.

He let his drool yo-yo from his lips, missing my feet by only inches, after which he giggled and called me names. Finally he let me up. I slapped grass from my jacket and pants, and pulled my shirt tail from my pants to shake out the fistful of dirt he had stuffed in my collar. I stood by him, nervous and red-faced from struggling, and when he suggested that we climb the monkey bars together, I followed him quietly to the kid's section of Jefferson Elementary. He climbed first, with small grunts, and for a second I thought of running but knew he would probably catch me—if not then, the next day. There was no way out of being a fifth grader—the daily event of running to teachers to show them your bloody nose. It was just a fact, like having lunch.

So I climbed the bars and tried to make conversation, first about the girls in our classroom and then about kickball. He looked at me smiling as if I had a camera in my hand, his teeth green like the underside of a rock, before he relaxed his grin into a simple gray line across his face. He told me to shut up. He gave me a hard stare and I looked away to a woman teacher walking to her car and wanted very badly to yell for help. She unlocked her door, got in, played with her face in the visor mirror while the engine warmed, and then drove off with blue smoke trailing. Frankie was watching me all along and when I turned to him, he laughed, "*Chale!* She can't help you, *ese.*" He moved closer to me on the bars and I thought he was going to hit me; instead he put his arm around my shoulder, squeezing firmly in friendship. "C'mon, chicken, let's be cool."

I opened my mouth and tried to feel happy as he told me what he was going to have for Thanksgiving. "My Mamma's got a turkey and ham, lots of potatoes, yams and stuff like that. I saw it in the refrigerator. And she says we gonna get some pies. Really, *ese.*"

Poor liar, I thought, smiling as we clunked our heads softly like good friends. He had seen the same afternoon program on TV as I had, one in which a woman in an apron demonstrated how to prepare a Thanksgiving dinner. I knew he would have tortillas and beans, a round steak maybe, and oranges from his backyard. He went on describing his Thanksgiving, then changed over to Christmas—the new bicycle, the clothes, the G.I. Joes. I told him that it sounded swell, even though I knew he was making it all up. His mother would in fact stand in line at the Salvation Army to come away hugging armfuls of toys that had been tapped back into shape by reformed alcoholics with veined noses. I pretended to be excited and asked if I could come over to his place to play after Christmas. "Oh, yeah, anytime," he said, squeezing my shoulder and clunking his head against mine.

When he asked what I was having for Thanksgiving, I told him that we would probably have a ham with pineapple on the top. My family was slightly better off than Frankie's, though I sometimes walked around with cardboard in my shoes and socks with holes big enough to be ski masks, so holidays were extravagant happenings. I told him about the scalloped potatoes, the candied yams, the frozen green beans, and the pumpkin pie.

His eyes moved across my face as if he were deciding where to hit me—nose, temple, chin, talking mouth—and then he lifted his arm from my shoulder and jumped from the monkey bars, grunting as he landed. He wiped sand from his knees while looking up and warned me not to mess around with him any more. He stared with such a great meanness that I had to look away. He warned me again and then walked away. Incredibly relieved, I jumped from the bars and ran looking over my shoulder until I turned onto my street.

Frankie scared most of the school out of its wits and even had girls scampering out of view when he showed himself on the playground. If he caught us without notice, we grew quiet and stared down at our shoes until he passed after a threat or two. If he pushed us down, we stayed on the ground with our eyes closed and pretended that we were badly hurt. If he riffled through our lunch bags, we didn't say anything. He took what he wanted, after which we sighed and watched him walk away peeling an orange or chewing big chunks of an apple.

Still, that afternoon when he called Mr. Koligian, our teacher, a foul name—we grew scared for him. Mr. Koligian pulled and tugged at his body until it was in his arms and then out of his arms as he hurled Frankie against the building. Some of us looked away because it was unfair. We knew the house he lived in: The empty refrigerator, the father gone, the mother in a sad bathrobe, the beatings, the yearnings for something to love. When the teacher manhandled him, we all wanted to run away, but instead we stared and felt shamed. Robert, Adele, Yolanda shamed; Danny, Alfonso, Brenda shamed; Nash, Margie, Rocha shamed. We all watched him flop about as Mr. Koligian shook and grew red from anger. We knew his house and, for some, it was the same one to walk home to: The broken mother, the indifferent walls, the refrigerator's glare which fed the people no one wanted.

Summer School

The summer before I entered sixth grade I decided to go to summer school. I had never gone, and it was either school or mope around the house with a tumbler of Kool-Aid and watch TV, flipping the channels from exercise programs to soap operas to game shows until something looked right.

My sister decided to go to summer school too, so the two of us hopped onto our bikes and rode off to Heaton Elementary, which was three miles away, and asked around until we were pointed to the right rooms. I ran off without saying good-bye to Debra.

These were the home rooms where the teachers would check roll, announce bulletins, and read us a story before we dashed off to other classes. That morning I came in breathing hard, smiling a set of teeth that were fit for an adult, and took a seat behind a fat kid named Yodelman so I couldn't be seen.

The teacher, whose name is forgotten, told us that summer school classes were all electives—that we could choose anything we wanted. She had written them on the blackboard, and from her list I chose science, history, German, and square dancing.

Little John, a friend from our street, sat across the room. I had not seen him at first, which miffed him because he thought I was playing stuck-up for some reason, and so he threw an acorn at me that bounced harmlessly off Yodelman's shoulder. Yodelman turned his head slowly, turtle-like, blinked his small dull eyes, and then turned his head back to the teacher who was telling us that we had to fill out cards. She had two monitors pass out pencils, and we hovered and strained over the card: Date of birth, address, grade, career goals. At the last one I thought for the longest time, pencil poised and somewhat worried, before I raised my hand to ask the teacher how to spell paleontology. Surprised, as if someone had presented her flowers, she opened her mouth, searched the ceiling with her eyes, and gave it a stab: p-a-y-e-n-t-o-l-o-g-y. I wrote it in uneven capitals and then wrote "bone collector" in the margin.

Little John glared at me, made a fist, and wet his lips. When class was dismissed he punched me softly in the arm and together the two of us walked out of class talking loudly, happy that we were together.

While Little John went to typing I went to science class. The teacher stood before us in a white shirt, yardstick in hand, surrounded by jars of animal parts floating in clear liquids. This scared me, as did a replica of a skeleton hanging like a frayed coat in the corner. On the first day we looked carefully at leaves in groups of threes, after which the teacher asked us to describe the differences.

"This one is dried up and this one is not so dried up," one kid offered, a leaf in each hand.

The teacher, who was kind, said that that was a start. He raised his yardstick and pointed to someone else.

From there I went to history, a class I enjoyed immensely because it was the first one ever in which I would earn an A. This resulted from reading thirty books—pamphlets to be more exact. I was a page turner, and my index finger touched each paragraph before the thumb peeled a new page, as I became familiar with Edison, Carnegie, MacArthur, Eli Whitney... At the end of the five-week summer school, the teacher would call me to the front of the class to tell about the books I had read. He stood behind the lectern, looking down at his watch now and then, and beamed at me like a flashlight.

"Who was Pike?"

"Oh, he was the guy that liked to go around in the mountains."

"Who was Genghis Khan?"

"He was a real good fighter. In China."

With each answer the teacher smiled and nodded his head at me. He smiled at the class and some of the students turned their heads away, mad that I knew so much. Little John made a fist and wet his lips.

From history we were released to the playground where we played softball, sucked on popsicles, and fooled around on the monkey bars. We returned to our classes sweating like the popsicles we had sucked to a rugged stick. I went to German where, for five weeks, we sang songs we didn't understand, though we loved them and loved our teacher who paraded around the room and closed his eyes on the high notes. On the best days he rolled up his sleeves, undid his tie, and sweated profusely as he belted out songs so loudly that we heard people pounding on the wall for quiet from the adjoining classroom. Still, he went on with great vigor:

Mein Hut der hat drei Ecken
Drei Ecken hat mein Hut
Und wenn er das nicht hatte
Dan war's auch nicht mein Hut

And we joined in every time, faces pink from a wonderful beauty that rose effortlessly from the heart.

I left, humming, for square dancing. Debra was in that class with me, fresh from science class where, she told me, she and a girlfriend had rolled balls of mercury in their palms to shine nickels, rings, earrings, before they got bored and hurled them at the boys. The mercury flashed on their shoulders, and they pretended to be shot as they staggered and went down to their knees.

Even though Debra didn't want to do it, we paired off the first day. We made ugly faces at each other as we clicked our heels, swished for a few steps, and clicked again.

It was in that class that I fell in love with my corner gal who looked like Haley Mills, except she was not as boyish. I was primed to fall in love because of the afternoon movies I watched on television, most of which were stories about women and men coming together, parting with harsh feelings, and embracing in the end to marry and drive big cars.

Day after day we'd pass through do-si-does, form Texas stars, spin, click heels, and bounce about the room, released from our rigid school children lives to let our bodies find their rhythm. As we danced I longed openly for her, smiling like a lantern and wanting very badly for her eyes to lock onto mine and think deep feelings. She swung around my arm, happy as the music, and hooked onto the next kid, oblivious to my yearning.

When I became sick and missed school for three days, my desire for her didn't sputter out. In bed with a comic book, I became dreamy as a cat and closed my eyes to the image of her allemanding left to *The Red River Valley*, a favorite of the class's, her long hair flipping about on her precious shoulders. By Friday I was well, but instead of going to school I stayed home to play "jump and die" with the neighbor kids—a game in which we'd repeatedly climb a tree and jump until someone went home crying from a hurt leg or arm. We played way into the dark.

On Monday I was back at school, stiff as new rope, but once again excited by science, history, the gutteral sounds of German, and square dancing! By Sunday I had almost forgotten my gal, so when I walked into class my heart was sputtering its usual tiny, blue flame. It picked up, however, when I saw the girls come in, pink from the afternoon heat, and line up against the wall. When the teacher clapped her hands, announced something or another, and asked us to pair off, my heart was roaring like a well-stoked fire as I approached a girl that *looked* like my girlfriend. I searched her face, but it wasn't her. I looked around as we galloped about the room but I couldn't spot her. Where is she? Is that her? I asked myself. No, no, my girlfriend has a cute nose. Well, then, is that her? I wondered girl after girl and, for a moment in the dizziness of spinning, I even thought my sister was my girlfriend. So it was. All afternoon I searched for *her* by staring openly into the faces of girls with long hair, and when class was dismissed I walked away bewildered that I had forgotten what the love of my life looked like. The next day I was desperate and stared even more boldly, until the teacher pulled me aside to shake a finger and told me to knock it off.

But I recovered from lost love as quickly as I recovered from jumping from trees, especially when it was announced, in the fourth week of classes, that there would be a talent show—that everyone was welcome to join in. I approached Little John to ask if he'd be willing to sing with me—*Michael Row the Boat Ashore, If I Had a Hammer*, or *Sugar Shack*—anything that would bring applause and momentary fame.

"C'mon, I know they'll like it," I whined at him as he stood in center field. He told me to leave him alone, and when a fly ball sailed in his direction he raced for it but missed by several feet. Two runs scored, and he turned angrily at me: "See what you did!"

I thought of square dancing with Debra, but I had the feeling that she would screw up her face into an ugly knot if I should ask. She would tell her friends and they would ride their bikes talking about me. So I decided that I'd just watch the show with my arms crossed.

The talent show was held on the lawn, and we were herded grade by grade into an outline of a horseshoe: The first and second grades sat Indian-style, the third and fourth graders squatted on their haunches, and the fifth and sixth graders stood with their arms across their chests. The first act was two girls—sisters I guessed—singing a song about weather: Their fingers made the shape of falling rain, their arching arms made rainbows, and finally their hands cupped around smiling faces made sunshine. We applauded like rain while some of the kids whistled like wind from a mountain pass.

This was followed with a skit about personal hygiene— bathing and brushing one's teeth. Then there was a juggling act, another singing duo, and then a jazz tap dancer who, because he was performing on the grass, appeared to be stamping mud off his shoes. After each act my eyes drifted to a long table of typewriters. What could they possibly be for? I asked myself. They were such commanding machines, big as boulders lugged from rivers. Finally, just as the tap routine was coming to an end, kids began to show up behind them to fit clean sheets of paper into the rollers. They adjusted their chairs as they looked at one another, whispering. A teacher called our attention to the typewriters and we whistled like mountain wind again.

"All summer we have practiced learning how to type," the teacher said in a clear, deliberate speech. "Not only have we learned to type letters, but also to sing with the typewriters. If you listen carefully, I am sure that you will hear songs that you are familiar with." She turned to the kids, whose hands rested like crabs on the keys, raised a pencil, and then began waving it around. Click—clickclick—click—click—click, and I recognized *The Star Spangled Banner*—and recognized Little John straining over his keyboard. Damn him, I thought, jealous that everyone was looking at him. They then played *Waltzing Matilda*, and this made me even angrier because it sounded beautiful and because Little John was enjoying himself. Click-click-click, and they were playing *Michael Row the Boat Ashore*, and this made me even more mad. I edged my way in front of Little John and, when he looked up, I made a fist and wet my lips. Smiling, he wet his own lips and shaped a cuss word, which meant we would have a fight afterward, when the music was gone and there were no typewriters to hide behind.

Desire

I suppose my desire for girls was keenest as I approached adolescence. These feelings were tender, like rope burns, and the slightest suggestion from a girl had me drifting about the school yard with great yearning. I'm thinking of my "object of desire," Mary Palacio, a skinny-legged Chicana with braces who had liked me in the fifth grade at Jefferson Elementary. But at that time I was quick-witted at dodgeball and football, and didn't have time for her. When I returned from recess I was steaming and grass-stained. I chewed grass and spat the wad of green while she and her girlfriends looked on. Still, her eyes went vacant with love, despite the fact that I didn't care.

In the sixth grade, however, my desire took a turn. I was in love with her and told my pillow so as I hugged it at night. I spoke to it—private and deep things—and it spoke back: "You're a neat guy, Gary." But there was a problem. She was by then in love with another guy, a seventh grader the rumor had it, and my love for her didn't bounce back like radar, even when I gave her, by way of a friend, a valentine which had a lollipop pressed with the words "You're a cutie!" The night before I had sat on my bed shivering from fear and weighing it all, unsure whether or not she would laugh, cry affectionately, or simply nibble at the lollipop while watching *Superman* or *The Three Stooges*. Still, it was worth a risk: I slipped the lollipop into an envelope and ran my tongue across the flap, pressing it closed. This, perhaps, was the most frightening, if not indelible, decision I had ever made. Rejection was what scared me.

The next day a friend who was in her class handed her the

envelope with the lollipop valentine. It was just before lunch, prior to the period when valentines would be handed out, and in my mind I witnessed again and again her reaction. She would be surprised and alive with deep feelings; she would laugh and tell her friends I was a fool; she would satisfy her sweet tooth. I suffered greatly as I waited for school to end. When it did I ran out to the playground, to the monkey bars, where I climbed to the top and waited for her to come out of her class and head for home. Kids scattered noisily and my stare frisked the area in search of her. Finally she emerged from the room with a girlfriend and they walked with their brown bags of valentines, and although she must have sensed I was somewhere—behind a back stop or the bricked archway of one of the classrooms—she didn't look up. She walked with her friend at her side, neither of them talking, and disappeared behind a building as she dragged my heart like a toy duck on a string. I hung upside down on the bars, blood riding to my head, and wished I were dead.

But I lived on, gained weight, and entered junior high school with Mary. She was still part of my conscious life. My eyes followed her about campus, observing her every detail. She swung a brown lunch bag twice a week; she ate in the cafeteria the rest of the days. She wore a knee-length coat, a furry blue one with a belt that was attached in the back with two brass buttons pressed with anchors. Her hair was styled in a Sassoon cut: Twiggy was big that year, with the English invasion of wide-wale cords, wide belts and cruelly pale lipstick from Yardley. Paisley was "the thing" in fall, and she wore paisley. Madras was hot in spring, and she wore madras. She joined the choir, and at the Christmas assembly she stood in the second row, third from the end, her voice carrying like a kite through the auditorium to where I sat in the back with the nobodys.

She left me to my own devices, one of which was to become a school cadet. On Fridays I wore my uniform that was clearly meant for an adult. My pants legs billowed in the slightest wind; the shirt pockets came down below my ribs almost to my belly button. Whereas Mary had become stylish and popular, a darling among the Chicana cliques, I drifted in the opposite direction to become a hall guard who paced up and down the corridor during lunch time. For a year's service, I earned a green ribbon that I pinned proudly to my shirt pocket that sagged like loose skin. I also earned sergeant stripes that year.

The next year, as an eighth grader, my love took a different turn. It was Judy Paredes, daughter of a wealthy baker in town, whose brother Ernie was in my platoon. As a squad leader I marched my line of men about the school yard: behind the backstop between basketball hoops through the sand of the track pit to behind a row of bushes, where I stopped the squad and ordered Ernie front and center. He walked stiffly up to me, his eyes unblinking but moist from the cold. I looked over his shoulder to the squad and barked an about face command: aaabbaht fah! I turned to Ernie, who had begun to blink and wrinkle his nose, and asked him if Judy liked me. I had gotten wind of this possibility from a girlfriend of a girlfriend of Judy's.

Ernie, whose face was marked with acne, stared straight at me until I couldn't stand it. I had to look away and my attention fell upon an old man working his way up the alley that ran the length of the school. He was pushing a shopping cart filled with cardboard and bottles. I looked into Ernie's face, bravely: 'Does she like me?"

He had known what was coming, so his response was quick: "Yeah, I think so. I saw her hugging her pillow just the other night." He stopped, looked down at his shoes, and then back up to me. "She called your name." Then he rushed intimate detail that I hadn't even asked for. 'You should see her on the speedboat. You should see her stomach. It's flat, real flat—like an anvil!"

My hair lit up. My underarms went moist and I could feel a thread of sweat lengthening. I looked away and again turned to the old man in the alley turning over in his hands a shiny object. So she's hugging her pillow, I thought. A clear sign. Surf's up. Groovy. Outta sight. Papa's got a brand new bag!

"Aabaaht fah!" I barked. Ernie returned to the squad, which I marched from the bushes to the track pit between the basketball hoops behind the backstop and back to the central campus where we were assembled into a platoon and the period ended with three rings of a bell.

That night I, too, hugged my pillow that I had dimpled with punches, soft punches, that made a face of sorts. I whispered to it; I spoke hushed secrets—that once I wanted to be a priest; that I stole from my mother's purse, dimes only. My brother, who was in the bunk above me, yelled at me to stop muttering. I slept with a big grin on my face.

The next day was a Friday, I remember, because I wore the cadet uniform my mother had bought for me at Walter Smith's after much snivelling and whining on my part. I wandered through central campus before first period looking for Judy. It was cold that morning but I hadn't worn a jacket because I wanted to display my two rows of ribbons: hall guard, leadership, parade, armory, and conduct. I also wanted to show off my staff sergeant rank, with my color guard cords looping my shoulder and dangling handsomely almost to my elbow.

I searched for her among the colonnades where she often whispered with a girlfriend. No luck. I stuck my head into the foyer where the girls hung out to gossip and trade sandwiches and to tease and poke at one another's stiff hairdos. Again no luck. From there I went to see if she was already standing at her first period door. She was there, in a furry white jacket that had been in style the previous year but was quite acceptable a year later. I wet my lips as I approached her slowly, but the words—the thick note pad of love I had composed the night before—failed to flutter open in some great wind at the back of my brain. I walked past her to the end of the hall to rethink my crippled plan. I looked over the balcony. There was Scott, my best friend, in his black stretch jeans and maroon socks that beamed brightly in the gray morning. He saw me and called to me to come down and trade sandwiches. I pretended not to hear his shouting and bent down to tie my shoes, after which I waddled a few steps on my haunches because I didn't want to explain to Scott what I was up to. While waddling, however, Judy turned to look at me as she was about to go into her class. Her face was indifferent to me, even in the awkward position I had dropped into. Soto the penguin. She didn't laugh, smirk, or raise an eyebrow in interest but only opened the door of the classroom and entered, leaving me, the penguin, at a standstill. I got up, embarrassed and shaken at finding myself so foolish, and ran down the stairwell to search out Scott.

At lunch there was a dance in the auditorium. An arena of students looked dully on, hands in pockets and cradling stacks of books, as three or four couples dazzled everyone by turning tenderly in a slow dance with their eyes closed. For slow music there was the Righteous Brothers, The Drifters, Mary Wells. For fast dancing there was the Supremes, The Spencer Davis Group, James Brown, Martha and the Vandellas, and the Kingsmen with their *Louie, Louie*. Then there was surfer music: The Beach Boys, Jan and Dean, the GTOs, but these groups were seldom played because they weren't revved up with brow-sweating soul. The Beatles and Herman's Hermits were also considered surfer music.

I went to the dance and threaded my way through the crowd in search of Judy. When I spotted her with a girlfriend, both of them hugging their books, I turned around and walked back to the door to collect my thoughts. What was I going to ask her? Should I be blunt and ask her for a dance? Then, suddenly as a baseball through a window, I realized that I couldn't dance. I had never danced, though I had studied the spastic quiverings of those couples on American Bandstand. But could I do the same? Fear caught like a chicken bone in my throat as I walked back to where she was standing. But she was gone. Another girl, a cafeteria-helper type, stood in her place. There was nothing for me to do but to watch those on the dance floor wheel to James Brown's *It's a Man's World*, since I didn't have the energy or right words to search out Judy. I stood there, thinking that I at least looked dazzling in my uniform, and let her go for that day.

And I let her go the next day, and the next day, because I found out it was Gary Perez the baseball stud, not Gary Soto the cadet, who made her hug her pillow and say crazy things. An innocent mistake, no doubt, but still I had to beat up her brother Ernie for pulling the moveable strings of my heart and making me look like a fool to myself. Punchpunchpunch during cadet period, and I was demoted to a private again because the teacher caught me stuffing leaves inside his shirt behind the bushes.

It's just something you have to do.

Saturday with Jackie

I remember one Saturday being chased from the house by my mother. She had asked me to empty my pants pockets of Kleenex and I wagged my head while reading the morning comics, telling her that I would. But I didn't. An hour later when she tugged her first load from the washer, she found it flecked with bits of Kleenex. She screamed from the garage and I hurried outside, remembering too late about cleaning out my pockets. When I looked back halfway down the street, she was standing on the porch with a pair of my jeans in her hands. I jogged looking back because my brother Rick had come to stand with her and I thought that maybe she was going to send him after me.

I sat at a curb at the end of the block peeling an orange when Jackie, a school friend, turned the corner with a rattling shopping cart. I called him, and he maneuvered toward my direction, squinting at me as if I were a fire. I got up and approached him with my hands in my back pockets and my jacket zipped to my throat and almost hurting.

"What's up?" I asked, as if I didn't know. On our street it was a practice to collect Coke bottles that could be traded in at liquor stores at a nickel apiece.

"Making money," he answered, simply.

We stood in the street talking nonsense for a few minutes before I asked if he wanted to walk downtown. He looked at his cart, which gleamed like stolen goods, and pursed his lips, looking worried.

"I shouldn't but let's go anyhow," he said. But first he rolled his shopping cart home while I waited at the curb. When he

returned he was smiling because he had sold the Coke
bottles—twelve of them—to his mother for four cents apiece, and
jingled his pockets like a big spender. We started up Angus
Street, looking around without talking. If we did talk, it was not
in sentences but single words or phrases.

"Look," I said on Washington Street, at a cat curled like a
stone in a pile of grass clippings. Jackie threw a chip of bark and
the cat turned on its side, stretched, and yawned like death.

"What the. . .!" Jackie said on Orchard Street, to a parked car
with one of its doors missing. We looked in to find stacks of
newspapers bundled and piled to the ceiling.

We walked without saying too much because talking ruined
the joy of noiseless minds. Jackie understood this, I understood
this, so we walked looking around like television cameras,
catching families sitting down to breakfast, a dog biting fleas
from his paws, a grandpa raking leaves, pomegranate trees
almost ready to steal from. We looked around while that endless
film wound behind our eyes.

At Rontell's Volvo on Divisadero we stopped to run our
fingers slowly across the shiny paint jobs and gawk at the
instrument panels of Jaguars. Since it was early, we tried opening
doors but they were all locked.

"This one's for me," Jackie said, pointing out a Jaguar with
gas caps on both back fenders.

We left there impressed, our minds racing with cars, and made
our way up Mariposa Street where we stopped at "the nun's
place." I told Jackie that when I went to St. John's Catholic
School I often passed the convent and, for my own reasons,
imagined the nuns, after a day of teaching and threatening kids
with erasers in firing position, would come home, pray, and head
to the backyard to play soccer with the altar boys. I would stand
at the fence, which was eight feet tall, and hear sounds like balls
being kicked, followed by restrained laughter.

From there we checked the telephone booths and Coke
machine for change at St. John's Cathedral, climbed into a tree
and threw rocks at the Southern Pacific, and dodged cars on "L"
Street on our way to the Fresno Mall. Not yet ten o'clock, the
mall was quiet with only a few merchants hurrying, in a sort of
panic, to their businesses; their faces looked waxen and their
suits were bright as the toys at Woolworths. There were a few

hobos, some kids like us, a man refilling a newspaper rack, a lone mother whose coat was like a soiled rug on her shoulders.

We ambled on, occasionally stopping to gaze in store windows, especially at clothing stores where we grew dreamy as incense looking at shirts, pants, belts, loafers—those wonderful things that were as far from us as Europe.

We bought doughnuts at Hart's Restaurant and ate them in silence at an outdoor fountain, with the film behind our eyes picking up speed when the stores began to open and mothers and daughters in colorful dresses hurried, almost in step, with big purses looped on their forearms. We ate the doughnuts, then bought popcorn at Penney's, and returned once again to the fountain where there were now more mothers and daughters, with an occasional son in clean clothes who looked stupid, and probably felt stupid, while his mother warned him with a stern finger to not get lost or fool around.

We looked at each other, wagged our heads in disgust, and called him in low voices, "sissy boy." Getting up, we walked up the mall toward the north end that was under construction with new stores coming up—clothing, import, jewelry, record, and china. We stopped in front of a boarded-up building, which was ready to be torn down to make way for offices, as the sign posted in the front said. There were few people shopping in the area, so we pried and pushed at the door until we could squeeze inside. Once inside, we looked around like astronauts on the moon. A shaft of sunlight, with its orbiting dust, shone from the roof and ended in a seizure of light far on the other side, where we made out desks, chairs, counters, an open elevator, and a broken mirror on the wall, its crack running like the border between Mexico and the United States. We made out mannequins, a hatrack, a pile of curtains, some empty boxes, and the octopus of a tangled chandelier resting on the ground. We took a few steps, with the film behind our eyes turning slowly, as we wanted to touch the mannequins. We walked carefully because of the dark. Broken glass crunched under our shoes; dust, thick as the first minute of snow, made us sneeze. We sensed spiders but we didn't find any swinging on their trapeze. We sensed mice but the only noises were from those things we knocked over. We walked like blind men, hands out and feeling the air, until we reached the mannequins and started back, each of us with one of them under his arm like a surf board. Jackie fell once, so that a finger chipped off, but mine was intact and even smiling when I squeezed it from the door into sunlight.

"It's a guy," I said to Jackie. "He's got a mustache—and check out the muscles." The mannequin was tall as Superman and his face looked like a composite drawing of Dick Tracy and Fabian.

Jackie brought out his mannequin whose wrist was limp and whose eyes were painted with feathery lashes. A merchant, who was standing at his window, winced in our direction. We pretended nonchalance and walked slowly around the building before running up the mall into an alley, where we hid behind boxes breathing hard and smiling from our adventure. When no one came to get us, we shouldered our mannequins and walked away, thinking that we could sell them. When no one came to mind, we decided to make them fight.

"You're an idiot," I screamed at his mannequin.

"You're a double idiot," Jackie said. He held his mannequin like a club and smacked mine right in the face, which cracked and chipped. I swung mine, and his mannequin's head fell off.

"You're a triple idiot," he threw at me, swinging his mannequin so that it thudded mine in the chest, almost knocking me down. I swung, then he swung, and I swung again and again, and he swung again and again, until only the arms were left, which we used as swords in our fight all the way back home.

The Small Faces

I was sixteen and unable to find a summer job, so instead of
moping around the house I volunteered to become a recreational
assistant for the City Parks Department. I had read about the
need for volunteers in the *Fresno Bee*. I called a phone number,
left my name with a woman, and waited several days before my
call was returned by the same woman who lauded my
goodheartedness before she came down to business.

"Young man, there are a number of schools and parks. Take
your time and just tell me which one sounds nice to you." She
read down the list and I almost shouted when she said "Emerson
Elementary."

"Emerson. I want to go there!"

"That one is still open," she said, and I could hear a pencil
scratching an imagined index card. The woman gave me the
name of Calvin Jones, the recreation leader, and said that I could
start Monday at six if I liked. She again thanked me for my
goodheartedness, asked me to spell my last name, and hung up.

That Monday, after dinner, I walked the four miles to
Emerson, across Belmont, Tulare, and Ventura Avenues, where
the houses, poor and dilapidated, slowly gave way to industry
and shops—bakery, auto parts stores, a tire company, machine
shop, and the import car dealer, Haron the Baron. There was a
house for every vacant lot, a working car for every car that was
rusting on flat tires. So this is what it's like, I thought. I walked
in wonder and in quiet happiness because this was the area where
I had spent my first six years. My entire family, including aunts,
uncles, father, brother, and even little sister, had gone to

Emerson Elementary for at least one year. I walked through the vacant lots that gleamed with glass, burst mattresses, gutted refrigerators, a TV like a large one-eyed robot without legs—all the wonderful treasures that kids like.

As I slowly approached Emerson I made out the screaming of kids at play. When I got closer I could see a line of them, wet and with their hands pressed together as if in prayer. They were shivering but anxious as they waited their turns at the "Slip & Slide," that long runway of plastic, to dive onto, chest first, its surface of beaded water. To my surprise the coach was a black man—surprise because, aside from garbage men, I had never seen a black person employed by the city. He was leaning against the chain link fence, gazing almost in wonder at the grass at his feet. I approached him and he looked at me slowly and without response. Smiling, I told him who I was, a summer volunteer. He wrinkled up his face: "Summer volunteer? No one said anything to me." He played with his chin, rubbing and pinching at his fuzzy goatee, and again gazed at his feet. Realizing that his welcome was unkind, if not rude, he burst out a hearty, "Well, it's good to have you here," and touched my shoulder. We exchanged names and bits of information, like I was a high school student and he was a college student.

We looked up together at the kids, all of them Mexican, all shiny in the twilight. One looked at me, curious about who I was, but the others had their eyes locked on the "Slip & Slide." I watched them for a while until I became uneasy at having nothing to do. Calvin stood watching the kids, though I sensed his thoughts were elsewhere. His brow lined with worry, then relaxed, then lined again, while his mouth, slightly puckered, moved as if he were getting ready to say something. But we leaned against the fence in silence, hands behind our backs holding onto the fence. After a while I braved a question. "What kind of programs do the kids have?" When I was their age, between five and eleven, my playground had crafts contests and baseball games, as well as swimming lessons.

Calvin pursed his lips, sighed, and jingled coins and keys in his pockets. "Well, Gary, we play a lot of dominoes." He pointed to a green shed, which he said was the game room. "We play over there." I followed his pointing arm to a picnic table. Next to the table stood a tree, thin as a hatrack, with only a few of its leaves moving in the breeze. But most were wilting and pale. I scanned the baseball field, the bungalows, and the school building itself. Even in the early evening the place looked dry and abandoned. I squinted hard and saw someone walking toward us, a girl about fourteen who was dressed in a T-shirt and cut off jeans. She stared at me and I stared back, unsmiling but interested because she wasn't bad looking. She clip-clopped in rubber sandals toward the line of kids where she bent to talk to one who seemed to be her younger brother. She looked up at me—or maybe Calvin—and several of the kids turned to look in our direction.

Calvin pushed away from the chain link fence and announced that time was up, the "Slip & Slide" had to be put away. He looked at his watch as he walked over to shut off the faucet. The kids moaned, begging him to turn it back on. Some took last dives, even as Calvin began rolling up one end of the plastic runway. Wanting something to do, I helped by coiling up the hose while the kids watched me with interest. Finally one asked me, "Who are you?" Without looking up, Calvin said my name and told them I was his recreational assistant. I tried to look friendly but grown up and serious too.

I asked the kid who looked like a cousin of mine what his name was, but he averted his eyes and ran away in the direction of the game room. Some other kids, after staring openly at me, ran after him while two left for home. Calvin and I walked together, with me dragging the hose and him the "Slip & Slide." He took the hose and told me to join the kids who sat at the table pounding their fists as if they wanted to eat. Joining them I again told them my name and still they paid me little attention. I tried again by telling them where I lived and what high school I went to.

"Are you a 'Mescan'?" the cousin look-alike asked.

I felt as if a spear had been thrown at my feet. I wanted to collar the kid for asking such a naked question, but I smiled, wagged my head, and told him that I was.

"Are you getting money for coming here?" another kid asked.

"No, maybe next year I can get a job," I answered feebly. I was embarrassed because I couldn't explain why I'd come to their playground as a volunteer. I was crumbling inside but on the outside I remained calm. Trying to be happy, I told the kids that

I didn't know how to play dominoes but maybe one of them could teach me.

"What's your name?" I asked the cousin look-alike.

"Alfonso." He offered no more information and lowered his head to pick at a sliver in his palm.

"And yours?" I asked, turning to an older boy about nine.

"Roberto. Alfonso's my brother." He was about to ask me a question but stopped. He looked away in the direction of Calvin who was returning with a coffee can of dominoes.

"What is it?" I coaxed him. But when Calvin was within earshot, I went silent and made an eager face because I wanted badly to be liked by these kids, as well as by Calvin. My eyes followed the coffee can as if it were a birthday cake or a present. Calvin dipped his hand into the coffee can and placed the dominoes face down. Roberto, the oldest of the kids there, helped turn them over while the two other kids, Marsha and Esteban, sat quietly watching. Alfonso ran a domino up his arm, all the while whining like a car turning a corner.

The game was interesting to me. Calvin won the first one but Roberto came back to win the second one. Grinning, Roberto challenged him to another but Calvin said that I should be given a chance to play. "You're just scared," Roberto taunted him. Calvin smiled back, shook his head, and stood up to look at a slow rattling truck, piled high with grass clippings and brush.

Roberto shoved the can at Alfonso, telling him to play with me, and ran toward a boy walking outside the fence with Coke bottles under his arms. Shamelessly, I turned to a seven-year-old Alfonso whose hand was already in the can scooping out dominoes, which he turned face down so the dots did not show. He smeared them with an open palm to mix them up, although they didn't circulate very well because he just moved them back and forth so they were in their original places when he stopped. I turned over a domino—a six. Alfonso turned over an eight, so he went first, slowly building a spine of dominoes.

"You do it like this," he said. He connected a four to a four that ran in a new direction. "And don't use your blank ones until you gotta." In the end Alfonso won, and wanting to try again I turned them over to mix them up.

I smiled, eager now that I understood the game. "Let's play another." Instead of answering me he swung his legs from under the table and ran to the game room, leaving a small impression of wet cut offs on the bench. He came back with a large four-square ball that was pressed to his chest like a bag of groceries.

"Let's play this."

With Marsha and Esteban, I joined him on the asphalt. He was only seven but he played like a tiger. I had to crumble to a knee on one shot and pick up my glasses from the ground when he hooked a shot at my feet and the ball rolled up my chest to my face. I won by two points. We played once more, and again I won. Marsha, a quiet girl with stringy hair, played next and I let her win a few points. She played without looking at me, and I played with my attention locked on her face: She looked like my sister at her age, except Marsha's eyes were greenish-brown and her disposition was soft and almost angelic.

I called her by her name every time she made a point or tried to make a difficult play.

"Good girl, Marsha. Almost, Marsha."

Esteban, her younger brother of about six, stepped into the square, and I played exaggeratedly slow, carrying the ball instead of tapping it across the line. He was like his sister, so shy that he wouldn't look at me; he looked downward at my feet and when I said "Good Esteban" his face wouldn't answer back with a smile or words. As with his sister, I let him get a few points in our game to eleven.

Alfonso was ready to play again, but Calvin, who had been talking with a neighbor at the fence, returned to say that it was closing time. Alfonso moaned. He bounced the ball in mock irritation. Marsha and Esteban ran to the gate without saying goodbye, although Marsha looked back at me just before crossing the street to her house.

I said good-bye to Calvin who thanked me for coming and said he hoped I'd come the next day. I left walking up Marsha's street and, although she didn't show herself, I sensed she was probably watching me from her porch. I walked quickly up the street whose houses were ill-kept and broken: ripped screen doors, dirt where grass once grew, and the paint fading into chalky dust. I followed the shortcut through vacant lots to Ventura Street on my way home.

Again, after dinner the next day, I walked the four miles to Emerson Elementary, all the while thinking of Marsha and her brother Esteban. I wondered about them, why they were so shy, who their father and mother were, how they were doing in school. When I arrived sweating from the long walk, Alfonso waved at me from the line of kids who were in line at the "Slip & Slide." Calvin was nowhere in sight.

"Where's Calvin?" I asked. Two kids pointed in the direction of the school. I wondered why he was over there and was irritated that he wasn't with the kids. He should be doing more, I thought. He's the one getting paid. But I let this drop from my mind and turned to say "Hi" to all the kids—six of them—who just looked at me or made playful bird noises at me. Calvin returned shortly and together we leaned against the fence in the shade of a sycamore. We watched them in silence before Calvin suggested that he and I go play dominoes.

"Now you kids mind yourselves," he warned them. Some made faces while others made bird noises and cow sounds. We walked slowly to the game room and, in spite of his disinterest in the kids, I still wanted to be his friend. I tried to start up a conversation about college.

"Is it really hard work?"

"Not really. Just algebra. I didn't do too well in math. Never did." We talked awhile about college but our talk slowly dwindled to phrases, solitary words, and finally nothing. We played three games and Calvin took the time to point out my errors after each loss. He then got up and said that he was going to put away the "Slip & Slide." I heard moans in the distance and the slap of feet running in the direction of the table, with Roberto shouting to the others, "I'm going to play him first."

"You're in trouble," I told Roberto who said that I'd be sorry. Squinting, I watched Calvin disappear into the school building and then lowered my attention to the scramble of dominoes. I smiled at Marsha and Esteban and pulled sticks of gum from my back pocket.

"This is good," I said. I held them fanned out like cards. "Take your pick." They did. And so did Roberto, Alfonso, and another boy by the name of Danny.

I played three games and lost them all. Tired of losing, I suggested to Marsha and Esteban that we could play two-square.

They swung their legs from under the bench and headed for the asphalt while I went to get the ball. We played several games. Again I let them get a few points and played so slowly that my movements were like a swimmer's under water. After this we played a made up game in which I bounced the ball into the air while they staggered underneath in an attempt to catch the ball. The higher I bounced it, the more they screwed up their faces and showed their tiny teeth, somewhat scared when the ball slapped their palms or bounced off their chests. With every attempt to catch the ball, I cooed, "Good, Marsha, 'atta boy, Esteban."

They played without once looking at me. I could have continued bouncing the ball, calling out, "It's high as a kite—get it," but the game had grown tiresome and I wanted another chance to play dominoes with Roberto, who was taunting me and chewing his gum loudly. I bounced the ball to Marsha, told her to play with her brother, and, rubbing my hands together, told Roberto he was in trouble, that he was dead, that he was going to be sorry that he ever came to the playground. Smiling, he made his own predictions, which were truer than mine. Again he won by luck and my mistakes. He rubbed his hands together, mocking me. Instead of playing again, I shoved the can to Roberto's friend, made a feeble joke, and joined Esteban and Marsha.

"Let's play some more!"

Again we played our made up game while I cried out, "It's high as a bird—get it," until Calvin walked slowly from the school building clapping, "Closing time." Marsha and Esteban ran to the gate on their way home, but this time Marsha didn't turn to look back with that wide-eyed look of "Who are you?" She crossed the street into the house with an orange tree and a dirt yard. When I passed her house that night I could make out a TV and a person I imagined to be her father, his face blue from sitting close to the screen.

The next day Calvin brought magazines for cutting out pictures to paste on milk carton collages. Only Marsha, Esteban, and Alfonso joined us. Trying to make them like me more, I again passed out chewing gum and life savers, which they cheered over and sucked with pleasure. Calvin refused these treats with a "no, no," and sat apart wearing his sun glasses, and thumbed through a magazine, stopping at ads for cars.

I worked with Marsha, helping her dot glue on the pictures, and turned to Esteban's collage to suggest that his needed some blues, maybe a sea or a picture of the sky. We found a bathtub, skyblue, with a little girl shampooing her shaggy dog. "This is funny," he said, and snipped it very carefully from the page.

"That's a good one," I beamed at him. I dotted glue on the back and held the clipping up like a fish for him to grab. He pasted it on the milk carton, stared at it, and made a half attempt to smile like the girl shampooing her dog.

I turned to Calvin. "What do you think?" He looked up slowly and smiled slowly. "Esteban, you're too much." We worked on the collages that day but on the next I brought a bag of pinto beans, which I spilled carefully like diamonds onto the table. I handed out chewing gum and jaw breakers as I explained that we were going to write out our names using beans. They sucked, chewed, rolled their gum and jaw breakers; they considered the beans, then my moving mouth, then the beans again.

"What for?" Alfonso asked.

I was caught off guard by this question. Almost laughing, I said, "Just to see if we can do it." I searched their faces, again almost laughing. "It could be fun—don't you think?"

They worked diligently as they glued the beans in the shape of their last names on cardboard. When they finished I asked them to dab each bean a different color of poster paint, delicately so the beans wouldn't fall off. Marsha and Esteban worked in silence although Alfonso whined that it was boring. But after awhile even he had grown absorbed and quiet as the other two. When Calvin, who had been hitting fly balls to Roberto and Danny, returned to the table, Alfonso was the first to point out his creation. Calvin smiled wide, like a light turned on, and said "That's beautiful, man." He ruffled Alfonso's hair and called him Picasso.

The next day I brought spray paint, some cans, and a box of macaroni shaped like wagon wheels. I poured the macaroni onto the table and explained, with animated enthusiasm, that we were going to make pencil holders from the cans; that we would spray-paint the cans, glue on the macaroni, and paint each macaroni with water colors.

The following day I brought coloring books which my

stepfather, a warehouseman for a book distributor, had given me. But there were no crayons in the game room, so we looked at the pictures—Bugs Bunny, Donald Duck, Felix the Cat—and chewed our gum. The next day I sneaked my little brother's crayons from the house and brought sheets of my sister's typing paper to make airplanes. We folded, drew snarling tiger mouths at the nose, and let the planes fly from our hands, all the while making the sound of jets.

In my third week at Emerson, Calvin was transferred to another playground, and William, a young white man in a bright yellow shirt and Bermuda shorts, stood in front of us saying that he was the new coach. He smiled at us for the longest time, hands on his hips, and then screwed up his face at the baseball field, the bungalows, and the school building. I was going to introduce myself as the recreational assistant, but knowing that he would say, "a what?" I said nothing and joined the kids at the table, where they were pounding their fists and singing, "We want dominoes, we want dominoes!" Trying to be friendly the new coach smiled, unlocked the game room, and clunked around. He returned with the coffee can and a football.

"How 'bout some catch?" he asked me, and I told him that it was too hot to play. Roberto and I played the first game, then Alfonso took my place. I took out jaw breakers from my pocket and offered them around, including to the coach who declined with a shake of his hand. We played dominoes while William hovered over us, one foot on the bench and arms crossed, and kept asking our names—Roberto, Alfonso, Danny, Marsha, Esteban, Gary.

Tired of winning, Roberto asked William if we could put out the "Slip & Slide."

"Slip & Slide?" he asked, as if surprised.

Roberto showed it to him in the game room, and together they tugged the "Slip & Slide" and the garden hose across the field to the strip of lawn between the bungalows. William stretched and smoothed it flat while Roberto connected the hose and sprayed in our direction to keep us at bay because he wanted to go first.

We jumped back, laughing. "We're going to get you," I yelled and he mocked me with my own words. William stepped aside, still smiling as if someone were ready to snap his picture, and

Roberto sprayed the "Slip & Slide" while looking over his shoulder to keep us back. But Alfonso ran, arms out and making plane noises, and he skidded across the plastic. Danny followed, with Marsha and Esteban skidding on their knees right behind him. I pulled off my shirt, flipped my rubber thongs at Roberto and buzzed low toward the plastic. When I skidded Roberto sprayed my face and yelled, "You're dead and wet." I glided across the plastic to the end, shocked by the cold water but happy and thinking it wasn't so bad.

Bloodworth

As early as kindergarten I had to bob and weave through fights—some I won and some I had to escape holding my nose like a doorknob. My first loss was in first grade over a red crayon. I was busy coloring flames on a neat four-sided house with a crooked chimney when a boy tried to pull the crayon away from me. I shoved him away, called him *menso* and proceeded to slash red flames at the house. But he came back with a girlish over-the-head punch that thudded on my back and, for a moment, stunned me by knocking the breath out of me. But I recovered quickly, turned around, and stabbed his forehead with the crayon, which left a small, red nick and made him run to the teacher, Miss Sue, a Chinese woman who consistently referred to me as "You, you."

Irate, because I had been a nuisance all week, Miss Sue shook me like a wet umbrella and pulled me toward the front of the classroom where she ordered the class, busy coloring, to return to their desks. Pushing her hair from her eyes, she asked, "How many of you want Gary to go to the principal's office?" I had been tugging to get free, but stopped when I saw all the hands leap up like flames into the air, even my girlfriend Rhonda's and my best friend Daryle's. I was shocked, then mad. My girlfriend! My best friend! So off I went screaming "No one likes me!" and, in the principal's office, could only think how I was going to beat up the whole class.

And I did, sooner or later, between second and third bases, in the bathroom while they stood at the urinals with their flies open like sails, and after school when I chased them home with rocks and bad words. So it went year after year, and perhaps my peak as a fighter came one week in spring the year I was a fifth grader when I was reportedly the gang leader of Mexicans who had beat up the Surfers. The Surfers, who were as poor as us and who probably had never seen the ocean in person, were sixth graders—and one of them was my brother Rick. I didn't find it strange because we often fought at home over the smallest thing, like a glass of Kool-Aid or a misplaced pencil, so when we met on the lawn one afternoon during lunch period, I had no bad feelings about trying to hit my brother in the nose. He made the decision to stand with the Surfers, and I made the decision to stand with the Mexicans. (I think it's something like becoming a Democrat or Republican—there are really no hard feelings if a relative belongs to a party different from your own.)

We met on the lawn and taunted them. "Hey, how's the surf. Your little deuce coupe, *ese*." They came back, "Eat your tacos and throw up." At that we lunged at them and sadly, since we were only fifth graders, we went down one after another from their sixth grader punches, holding our jaws and wiping our hurt noses. Lucky for us, I suppose, a teacher was walking toward the knot of onlookers; and the Surfers scattered while we ran to the jungle gym where we bared our teeth at one another to see if they were all right.

After lunch, while Mrs. Sloan read us *Pinocchio* and the class grew dreamy as we listened with heads pillowed in folded arms, I was called by the loud speaker on the wall next to the flag. The speaker crackled, buzzed, breathed hard, crackled some more, and finally spoke: "Please send Gary Soto to the principal's office immediately." I raised my head from my arms, looked around as everyone looked at me, and left the room wondering what I had done wrong. At the office a mother was there with one of the Surfers whose eyes were red from crying, and as I stepped into the principal's office, scared at the possibility of a paddling, the Surfer cried out, "That's him. He's the leader." Mr. Buckalew, usually so kind, frowned at me as the Surfer went loose-lipped; the mother wrung her hands and told Mr. Buckalew that her son had a heart condition, that any day he could die. I listened without saying anything but thought we were going to have to whip this "fink." After the mother and son had gone breathless from complaining, the principal turned and asked me if any of it was true.

"They're lying," I lied, with a generous wide-eyed innocence. "Really, Mr. Buckalew."

But in the end I leaned against his desk for a paddling, and the Surfer transferred to another school district when we chased him home for being a fink.

Hard times. All through elementary and junior high school, it was bob and weave, jab and stick. Only in high school did I get a chance to rest between rounds. I was amazed at the calm, almost pastoral, atmosphere of Roosevelt High and, for a while, was pleased to hover over tuna sandwiches during lunchtime without the worry of being jumped from behind. During the three years there I would only get into eight fights—the strangest one was with a 1963 Ford Falcon that tried to run me over as I crossed the street on my way to school. I kicked the car door, then the driver when he got out of his car, before I ran away to look for help.

Longing for the "good times," I joined the wrestling team to exercise my combative genes. Wrestling is a difficult sport that demands top notch conditioning, followed by speed, desire, and tooth-grinding meanness. During the first week of training we ran miles, did push-ups and sit-ups until we hurt, and practiced take-downs and half nelsons. We worked out in the "oven," a fifteen by thirty foot padded room, in which an overhead heater was turned on so we could sweat to lose weight. By the end of a two-hour workout, the room was puddled with sweat and so fogged that it was impossible to see across the room. We practiced with the intention of hurting each other, and Coach DeCarlo made no bones about it.

"When you get in there, don't be a damned fish. You're men, now. When you get him down, throw your chin into his back. Hurt him—or don't come back."

We all came back, either as victors or losers, and, if the latter, practiced even more fiercely to prove ourselves the next time. We wanted to hear the coach call us "animals," and smile with pride.

I wrestled for three years at the one-hundred-three weight class and my record was not particularly sparkling: Twenty-four wins, eleven losses. Just an average wrestler. I earned three letters but no ribbons or pins to dangle from a letterman's jacket. Still, I was loyal. I worked hard. I ran the miles, did the push-ups and sit-ups until I hurt, and by the end of the three years of wrestling

I was in the best condition I would ever enjoy. If I lifted my shirt at my brothers, I could blink a row of taut muscles—blink, "Don't mess with me," or "Stay back, Jack."

One night, in my third year, my mother decided to watch me wrestle. My family had taken little interest in my athletics and, in fact, had discouraged me from going out for the team because it meant expense: Insurance (five dollars), a check-up (seven dollars), and one knee pad (two dollars and fifty cents). Then there was the doctor bill of ten dollars for the blood poisoning I got from a scratch while wrestling. With the last, my mother kept saying, "No, it's nothing," even when I showed her a tangle of red veins that ran from my hand to my chest. I went to bed thinking about Jesus, but when I woke the next morning I was thinking of Dr. Welby, Dr. Kildare—anyone! I showed my veins to Mom again, and she said, "Well, OK, if we have to." She put down her coffee cup, dabbed lipstick on her cheeks and lips the color of my veins, and drove me to the doctor's. When I took off my shirt, his brow went dark with lines as he said, "This one's a dilly." He probed my armpit until it hurt and then set a row of injections on a stainless steel tray.

The night my mom decided to watch me wrestle, our match was with the perennial powerhouse, Madera High—and that night I was to face Bloodworth. His name was appropriate, since he was a city champion prone to head slapping and smearing his opponent's face into the mat before he turned him over to show him the "lights"—the overhead lights we'd look up at as the referee counted.

There were a few spectators in the gymnasium that night. At Roosevelt High few sat together, even if they came together as boyfriend and girlfriend, brothers, close friends, or relatives. Wrestling at Roosevelt was a sport you watched by yourself with a ten-cent bag of Corn Nuts you munched quicker and harder when a wrestler was on the edge of being pinned.

My mother arrived just a few minutes before the varsity team was called out. I spied her from behind the door where the team had lined up by weight. She stepped carefully into the bleachers, looked around, and then sat quietly in about the fourth row, smoothing her dress as if she were at a restaurant.

Called out by our coach, we ran gingerly and in step to circle the mat shouting: R-O-O-S-E-V-E-L-T. After that we clapped, dropped to the mat for neck bridges and leg stretches, and stood up again to practice take-downs. We huddled together again, shouted "Let's do it!" and broke away clapping as we turned to the folding chairs that faced the mat.

Madera was then called out and they followed with a similar routine.

I was nervous. I kept bouncing lightly on my toes and jingling my arms at my sides, all along knowing that I would be pinned. I knew Bloodworth was going to win, but I had to stay off my back and not see "the lights." I bounced around and jingled my arms. I adjusted my headgear and repositioned my one knee pad, on which I had notched my wins and losses with a Bic pen. The coach came up to me, clipboard in hand, and asked me how I felt. OK, I told him, although my mouth was dry and my stomach had that feeling—a sense of nausea that issued from fear. Without looking at him, I knew he was searching my face and wondering, "Can he do it?"

The buzzer sounded for the first match. Mike Brooks, our ninety-five-pounder who had a mean grip and was our best wrestler that year, approached the mat looking vacantly at the referee as he explained the rules we all knew. They shook hands, backed away, and when the buzzer sounded, Mike dangled his arms in front of his opponent as he waddled toward him. He grabbed his wrist, yanked, pushed, and yanked again and the opponent was on the mat, head arched back as he tried to get up. A two-point take-down was not enough for Mike, so he hammered his chin into his opponent's back. The other wrestler grunted to his knees, but Mike slipped his leg under his opponent's and shoved an elbow into his back with the intention of working him on a cradle. He pulled on an arm until it gave, and within seconds the opponent was on his back trying to bridge his way out of trouble, and within another few seconds he was looking up at "the lights," as the referee slammed his hand on the mat. Mike leaped off him and looked at the clock: Thirty-four seconds were left in the round. They shook hands and I could make out Mike saying, "Good match."

Liar, I thought. The guy was terrible. That quick pin won't help me out because Bloodworth will be upset at how quickly one of his teammates had gone down. I searched the bleachers and found Mom searching her purse for gum, a cigarette perhaps. The few spectators there were untwisting bags for Corn Nuts, readying for a good time.

The buzzer sounded. I approached the mat as my teammates stood up from their chairs to clap and shower me with, "C'mon, Gary. Stick him."

I approached the mat, looked at the referee moving his mouth, and shook hands with Bloodworth. We backed away two steps, each of us looking intensely at the other, and waited for the "Readyyyyy, wrestle." When it came I waddled toward Bloodworth with my arms dangling in front of me, in a parody of Mike's style. We locked heads together, pushed and yanked, and separated. I was already breathing hard, just from a few friendly shoves, and my ear, despite the headgear, felt raw from banging our heads together. We searched each other's faces and waddled toward one another, arms dangling. When he teased me with a leg, I decided, "Well, hell, why not," and scooted on my knees to grab his foot in a half-hearted attempt at a take-down. He ripped his forearm across my face. It hurt as he twisted my head and, consequently, my neck. He took me down, but I got up to my knees almost immediately to search out the clock, then the faces in the bleachers—faces that were busy going to town on Corn Nuts. I rose to my knees, then fell, but rose again when the buzzer sounded the end of the round. I stood up breathing hard, hands on hips as I circled the mat to stall for time and a precious breath of air. The referee asked Bloodworth to choose between heads or tails as he tossed a coin in the air. Heads, he called, and heads it was. He chose top. I circled around the mat one more time and then threw myself on the mat, on all fours. He set his grip on my elbow and around my waist, and I could feel his trembling—certainly from the rush of adrenaline. When the whistle sounded I tried to snap up into a standing position but was thrown down. I crawled, snail-like, my face smearing the mat with a moist nose, and could feel him trying to push his hand over my neck and across the back of my head in a half nelson. He pushed at my head, sweated on my head, breathed foully on my head. Bent down, the referee shouted at me to quit stalling—an insult, because I *was* trying to get to my knees. Grunting, I rose up on my padded knee and, for a second, it looked like I might even make it to two knees when Bloodworth slammed me into the mat and I continued to snail, nose pressed moist into the mat.

Just as I looked up to the clock, Bloodworth slipped his leg around mine and pulled at my arm in an attempt to roll me into the "cradle." "Thank God it's almost over," I thought as I grunted and gritted my teeth. But the buzzer sounded and I was released. I got up slowly, threw off my headgear whose earmuffs had worked their way across my eyes, and walked around the mat with hands on hips and breathing hard. I searched the bleachers and the spectators were finishing up their first bags of Corn Nuts. My Mom, with a clenched fist and a strained face, was yelling, "C'mon, *m'ijo*, kill him." Some of my teammates clapped their hands softly and threw out words of encouragement while others bowed their heads and looked at their feet.

Bloodworth was already on all fours and poised beautifully, eyes straight ahead like a horse's, when I plopped down on my knees to set my grip around his elbow and stomach. When the whistle sounded I pulled to my left, then quickly pushed him to the mat where he "snailed" to rise to his feet as I hung on thinking that I might not be pinned, that maybe I might even win. No sooner did such ideas snap from one brain cell to the next than Bloodworth rose to one knee, then the other knee, before he shot straight up like King Kong with me hanging desperately to his waist, as if I were begging him to stay. He slapped my hands away, turned, and ripped a forearm across my face while he took me down where he proceeded to tuck my arm into a half chicken wing, then into a full chicken wing before he rolled me slowly over on my back, and I glimpsed the wincing glare of overhead lights, and the spectators with their Corn Nuts, and the coach banging his clipboard against his thigh, and my teammates ripping their fingernails with their teeth, and my Mom standing up and yelling, "Hurt him, *m'ijo*. Kill him. Right now!"

I was pinned with forty-four seconds left of the third round. I got up breathing hard, head bowed, as I circled the mat. I shook hands with Bloodworth without looking up, returned to my folding chair and my teammates patting my shoulders, and sat down to towel off and watch Rhinehardt, our one-hundred-and-twelve, roll around the mat. While he was being turned over to see the lights, my Mom called from the bleachers, "M'ijo. M'ijo, do you want some gum?" Turning around, I saw that she had torn a piece of Juicy Fruit into halves and was holding it up like a goldfish. "Here, son. Catch." She threw it from the bleachers, and I opened my hands for its small sweetness.

One Last Time

Yesterday I saw the movie *Gandhi* and recognized a few of the people—not in the theater but in the film. I saw my relatives, dusty and thin as sparrows, returning from the fields with hoes balanced on their shoulders. The workers were squinting, eyes small and veined, and were using their hands to say what there was to say to those in the audience with popcorn and Cokes. I didn't have anything, though. I sat thinking of my family and their years in the fields, beginning with Grandmother who came to the United States after the Mexican revolution to settle in Fresno where she met her husband and bore children, many of them. She worked in the fields around Fresno, picking grapes, oranges, plums, peaches, and cotton, dragging a large white sack like a sled. She worked in the packing houses, Bonner and Sun-Maid Raisin, where she stood at a conveyor belt passing her hand over streams of raisins to pluck out leaves and pebbles. For over twenty years she worked at a machine that boxed raisins until she retired at sixty-five.

Grandfather worked in the fields, as did his children. Mother also found herself out there when she separated from Father for three weeks. I remember her coming home, dusty and so tired that she had to rest on the porch before she trudged inside to wash and start dinner. I didn't understand the complaints about her ankles or the small of her back, even though I had been in the grape fields watching her work. With my brother and sister I ran in and out of the rows; we enjoyed ourselves and pretended not to hear Mother scolding us to sit down and behave ourselves. A few years later, however, I caught on when I went to pick grapes rather than play in the rows.

Mother and I got up before dawn and ate quick bowls of cereal. She drove in silence while I rambled on how everything was now solved, how I was going to make enough money to end our misery and even buy her a beautiful copper tea pot, the one I had shown her in Long's Drugs. When we arrived I was frisky and ready to go, self-consciously aware of my grape knife dangling at my wrist. I almost ran to the row the foreman had pointed out, but I returned to help Mother with the grape pans and jug of water. She told me to settle down and reminded me not to lose my knife. I walked at her side and listened to her explain how to cut grapes; bent down, hands on knees, I watched her demonstrate by cutting a few bunches into my pan. She stood over me as I tried it myself, tugging at a bunch of grapes that pulled loose like beads from a necklace. "Cut the stem all the way," she told me as last advice before she walked away, her shoes sinking in the loose dirt, to begin work on her own row.

I cut another bunch, then another, fighting the snap and whip of vines. After ten minutes of groping for grapes, my first pan brimmed with bunches. I poured them on the paper tray, which was bordered by a wooden frame that kept the grapes from rolling off, and they spilled like jewels from a pirate's chest. The tray was only half filled, so I hurried to jump under the vines and begin groping, cutting, and tugging at the grapes again. I emptied the pan, raked the grapes with my hands to make them look like they filled the tray, and jumped back under the vine on my knees. I tried to cut faster because Mother, in the next row, was slowly moving ahead. I peeked into her row and saw five trays gleaming in the early morning. I cut, pulled hard, and stopped to gather the grapes that missed the pan; already bored, I spat on a few to wash them before tossing them like popcorn into my mouth.

So it went. Two pans equaled one tray—or six cents. By lunchtime I had a trail of thirty-seven trays behind me while mother had sixty or more. We met about halfway from our last trays, and I sat down with a grunt, knees wet from kneeling on dropped grapes. I washed my hands with the water from the jug, drying them on the inside of my shirt sleeve before I opened the paper bag for the first sandwich, which I gave to Mother. I dipped my hand in again to unwrap a sandwich without looking at it. I took a first bite and chewed it slowly for the tang of mustard. Eating in silence I looked straight ahead at the vines, and only when we were finished with cookies did we talk.

"Are you tired?" she asked.

"No, but I got a sliver from the frame," I told her. I showed her the web of skin between my thumb and index finger. She wrinkled her forehead but said it was nothing.

"How many trays did you do?"

I looked straight ahead, not answering at first. I recounted in my mind the whole morning of bend, cut, pour again and again, before answering a feeble "thirty-seven." No elaboration, no detail. Without looking at me she told me how she had done field work in Texas and Michigan as a child. But I had a difficult time listening to her stories. I played with my grape knife, stabbing it into the ground, but stopped when Mother reminded me that I had better not lose it. I left the knife sticking up like a small, leafless plant. She then talked about school, the junior high I would be going to that fall, and then about Rick and Debra, how sorry they would be that they hadn't come out to pick grapes because they'd have no new clothes for the school year. She stopped talking when she peeked at her watch, a bandless one she kept in her pocket. She got up with an *"Ay, Dios,"* and told me that we'd work until three, leaving me cutting figures in the sand with my knife and dreading the return to work.

Finally I rose and walked slowly back to where I had left off, again kneeling under the vine and fixing the pan under bunches of grapes. By that time, 11:30, the sun was over my shoulder and made me squint and think of the pool at the Y.M.C.A. where I was a summer member. I saw myself diving face first into the water and loving it. I saw myself gleaming like something new, at the edge of the pool. I had to daydream and keep my mind busy because boredom was a terror almost as awful as the work itself. My mind went dumb with stupid things, and I had to keep it moving with dreams of baseball and would-be girlfriends. I even sang, however softly, to keep my mind moving, my hands moving.

I worked less hurriedly and with less vision. I no longer saw that copper pot sitting squat on our stove or Mother waiting for it to whistle. The wardrobe that I imagined, crisp and bright in the closet, numbered only one pair of jeans and two shirts because, in half a day, six cents times thirty-seven trays was two dollars and twenty-two cents. It became clear to me. If I worked eight hours, I might make four dollars. I'd take this, even gladly, and walk downtown to look into store windows on the mall and long for the bright madras shirts from Walter Smith or Coffee's, but settling for two imitation ones from Penney's.

That first day I laid down seventy-three trays while Mother had a hundred and twenty behind her. On the back of an old envelope, she wrote out our numbers and hours. We washed at the pump behind the farm house and walked slowly to our car for the drive back to town in the afternoon heat. That evening after dinner I sat in a lawn chair listening to music from a transistor radio while Rick and David King played catch. I joined them in a game of pickle, but there was little joy in trying to avoid their tags because I couldn't get the fields out of my mind: I saw myself dropping on my knees under a vine to tug at a branch that wouldn't come off. In bed, when I closed my eyes, I saw the fields, yellow with kicked up dust, and a crooked trail of trays rotting behind me.

The next day I woke tired and started picking tired. The grapes rained into the pan, slowly filling like a belly, until I had my first tray and started my second. So it went all day, and the next, and all through the following week, so that by the end of thirteen days the foreman counted out, in tens mostly, my pay of fifty-three dollars. Mother earned one hundred and forty-eight dollars. She wrote this on her envelope, with a message I didn't bother to ask her about.

The next day I walked with my friend Scott to the downtown mall where we drooled over the clothes behind fancy windows, bought popcorn, and sat at a tier of outdoor fountains to talk about girls. Finally we went into Penney's for more popcorn, which we ate walking around, before we returned home without buying anything. It wasn't until a few days before school that I let my fifty-three dollars slip quietly from my hands, buying a pair of pants, two shirts, and a maroon T-shirt, the kind that was in style. At home I tried them on while Rick looked on enviously; later, the day before school started, I tried them on again wondering not so much if they were worth it as who would see me first in those clothes.

Along with my brother and sister I picked grapes until I was fifteen, before giving up and saying that I'd rather wear old clothes than stoop like a Mexican. Mother thought I was being stuck-up, even stupid, because there would be no clothes for me in the fall. I told her I didn't care, but when Rick and Debra rose at five in the morning, I lay awake in bed feeling that perhaps I had made a mistake but unwilling to change my mind. That fall Mother bought me two pairs of socks, a packet of colored T-shirts, and underwear. The T-shirts would help, I thought, but who would see that I had new underwear and socks? I wore a new T-shirt on the first day of school, then an old shirt on Tuesday, than another T-shirt on Wednesday, and on Thursday an old Nehru shirt that was embarrasingly out of style. On Friday I changed into the corduroy pants my brother had handed down to me and slipped into my last new T-shirt. I worked like a magician, blinding my classmates, who were all clothes conscious and small-time social climbers, by arranging my wardrobe to make it seem larger than it really was. But by spring I had to do something—my blue jeans were almost silver and my shoes had lost their form, puddling like black ice around my feet. That spring of my sixteenth year, Rick and I decided to take a labor bus to chop cotton. In his old Volkswagen, which was more noise than power, we drove on a Saturday morning to West Fresno—or Chinatown as some call it—parked, walked slowly toward a bus, and stood gawking at the winos, toothy blacks, Okies, *Tejanos* with gold teeth, whores, Mexican families, and labor contractors shouting "Cotton" or "Beets," the work of spring.

We boarded the "Cotton" bus without looking at the contractor who stood almost blocking the entrance because he didn't want winos. We boarded scared and then were more scared because two blacks in the rear were drunk and arguing loudly about what was better, a two-barrel or four-barrel Ford carburetor. We sat far from them, looking straight ahead, and only glanced briefly at the others who boarded, almost all of them broken and poorly dressed in loudly mismatched clothes. Finally when the contractor banged his palm against the side of the bus, the young man at the wheel, smiling and talking in Spanish, started the engine, idled it for a moment while he adjusted the mirrors, and started off in slow chugs. Except for the windshield there was no glass in the windows, so as soon as we were on the rural roads outside Fresno, the dust and sand began to be sucked into the bus, whipping about like irate wasps as the gravel ticked about us. We closed our eyes, clotted up our mouths that wanted to open with embarrassed laughter because we couldn't believe we were on that bus with those people and the dust attacking us for no reason.

When we arrived at a field we followed the others to a pickup where we each took a hoe and marched to stand before a row. Rick and I, self-conscious and unsure, looked around at the others who leaned on their hoes or squatted in front of the rows, almost all talking in Spanish, joking, lighting cigarettes—all waiting for the foreman's whistle to begin work. Mother had explained how to chop cotton by showing us with a broom in the backyard.

"Like this," she said, her broom swishing down weeds. "Leave one plant and cut four—and cut them! Don't leave them standing or the foreman will get mad."

The foreman whistled and we started up the row stealing glances at other workers to see if we were doing it right. But after awhile we worked like we knew what we were doing, neither of us hurrying or falling behind. But slowly the clot of men, women, and kids began to spread and loosen. Even Rick pulled away. I didn't hurry, though. I cut smoothly and cleanly as I walked at a slow pace, in a sort of funeral march. My eyes measured each space of cotton plants before I cut. If I missed the plants, I swished again. I worked intently, seldom looking up, so when I did I was amazed to see the sun, like a broken orange coin, in the east. It looked blurry, unbelievable, like something not of this world. I looked around in amazement, scanning the eastern horizon that was a taut line jutted with an occasional mountain. The horizon was beautiful, like a snapshot of the moon, in the early light of morning, in the quiet of no cars and few people.

The foreman trudged in boots in my direction, stepping awkwardly over the plants, to inspect the work. No one around me looked up. We all worked steadily while we waited for him to leave. When he did leave, with a feeble complaint addressed to no one in particular, we locked up smiling under straw hats and bandanas.

By 11:00, our lunch time, my ankles were hurting from walking on clods the size of hardballs. My arms ached and my face was dusted by a wind that was perpetual, always busy whipping about. But the work was not bad, I thought. It was better, so much better, than picking grapes, especially with the hourly wage of a dollar twenty-five instead of piece work. Rick and I walked sorely toward the bus where we washed and drank water. Instead of eating in the bus or in the shade of the bus, we kept to ourselves by walking down to the irrigation canal that ran the length of the field, to open our lunch of sandwiches and crackers. We laughed at the crackers, which seemed like a cruel joke from our Mother, because we were working under the sun and the last thing we wanted was a salty dessert. We ate them anyway and drank more water before we returned to the field, both of us limping in exaggeration. Working side by side, we talked and laughed at our predicament because our Mother had warned us year after year that if we didn't get on track in school we'd have to work in the fields and then we would see. We mimicked Mother's whining voice and smirked at her smoky view of the future in which we'd be trapped by marriage and screaming kids. We'd eat beans and then we'd see.

Rick pulled slowly away to the rhythm of his hoe falling faster and smoother. It was better that way, to work alone. I could hum made-up songs or songs from the radio and think to myself about school and friends. At the time I was doing badly in my classes, mainly because of a difficult stepfather, but also because I didn't care anymore. All through junior high and into my first year of high school there were those who said I would never do anything, be anyone. They said I'd work like a donkey and marry the first Mexican girl that came along. I was reminded so often, verbally and in the way I was treated at home, that I began to believe that chopping cotton might be a lifetime job for me. If not chopping cotton, then I might get lucky and find myself in a car wash or restaurant or junkyard. But it was clear; I'd work, and work hard.

I cleared my mind by humming and looking about. The sun was directly above with a few soft blades of clouds against a sky that seemed bluer and more beautiful than our sky in the city. Occasionally the breeze flurried and picked up dust so that I had to cover my eyes and screw up my face. The workers were hunched, brown as the clods under our feet, and spread across the field that ran without end—fields that were owned by corporations, not families.

I hoed trying to keep my mind busy with scenes from school and pretend girlfriends until finally my brain turned off and my thinking went fuzzy with boredom. I looked about, no longer mesmerized by the beauty of the landscape, no longer wondering if the winos in the fields could hold out for eight hours, no longer dreaming of the clothes I'd buy with my pay. My eyes followed my chopping as the plants, thin as their shadows, fell with each strike. I worked slowly with ankles and arms hurting, neck stiff, and eyes stinging from the dust and the sun that glanced off the field like a mirror.

By quitting time, 3:00, there was such an excruciating pain in my ankles that I walked as if I were wearing snowshoes. Rick laughed at me and I laughed too, embarrassed that most of the men were walking normally and I was among the first timers who had to get used to this work. "And what about you, wino," I came back at Rick. His eyes were meshed red and his long hippie hair was flecked with dust and gnats and bits of leaves. We placed our hoes in the back of a pickup and stood in line for our pay, which was twelve fifty. I was amazed at the pay, which was the most I had ever earned in one day, and thought that I'd come back the next day, Sunday. This was too good.

Instead of joining the others in the labor bus, we jumped in the back of a pickup when the driver said we'd get to town sooner and were welcome to join him. We scrambled into the truck bed to be joined by a heavy-set and laughing *Tejano* whose head was shaped like an egg, particularly so because the bandana he wore ended in a point on the top of his head. He laughed almost demonically as the pickup roared up the dirt path, a gray cape of dust rising behind us. On the highway, with the wind in our faces, we squinted at the fields as if we were looking for someone. The *Tejano* had quit laughing but was smiling broadly, occasionally chortling tunes he never finished. I was scared of him, though Rick, two years older and five inches taller, wasn't. If the *Tejano* looked at him, Rick stared back for a second or two before he looked away to the fields.

I felt like a soldier coming home from war when we rattled into Chinatown. People leaning against car hoods stared, their necks following us, owl-like; prostitutes chewed gum more ferociously and showed us their teeth; Chinese grocers stopped brooming their storefronts to raise their cadaverous faces at us. We stopped in front of the Chi Chi Club where Mexican music blared from the juke box and cue balls cracked like dull ice. The *Tejano*, who was dirty as we were, stepped awkwardly over the side rail, dusted himself off with his bandana, and sauntered into the club.

Rick and I jumped from the back, thanked the driver who said *de nada* and popped his clutch, so that the pickup jerked and coughed blue smoke. We returned smiling to our car, happy with the money we had made and pleased that we had, in a small way, proved ourselves to be tough; that we worked as well as other men and earned the same pay.

We returned the next day and the next week until the season was over and there was nothing to do. I told myself that I wouldn't pick grapes that summer, saying all through June and July that it was for Mexicans, not me. When August came around and I still had not found a summer job, I ate my words, sharpened my knife, and joined Mother, Rick, and Debra for one last time.

Black Hair

There are two kinds of work: One uses the mind and the other uses muscle. As a kid I found out about the latter. I'm thinking of the summer of 1969 when I was a seventeen-year-old runaway who ended up in Glendale, California, to work for Valley Tire Factory. To answer an ad in the newspaper I walked miles in the afternoon sun, my stomach slowly knotting on a doughnut that was breakfast, my teeth like bright candles gone yellow.

I walked in the door sweating and feeling ugly because my hair was still stiff from a swim at the Santa Monica beach the day before. Jules, the accountant and part owner, looked droopily through his bifocals at my application and then at me. He tipped his cigar in the ashtray, asked my age as if he didn't believe I was seventeen, but finally after a moment of silence, said, "Come back tomorrow. Eight-thirty."

I thanked him, left the office, and went around to the chain link fence to watch the workers heave tires into a bin; others carted uneven stacks of tires on hand trucks. Their faces were black from tire dust and when they talked—or cussed—their mouths showed a bright pink.

From there I walked up a commercial street, past a cleaners, a motorcycle shop, and a gas station where I washed my face and hands; before leaving I took a bottle that hung on the side of the Coke machine, filled it with water, and stopped it with a scrap of paper and a rubber band.

The next morning I arrived early at work. The assistant foreman, a potbellied Hungarian, showed me a timecard and how to punch in. He showed me the Coke machine, the locker room with its slimy shower, and also pointed out the places where I shouldn't go: The ovens where the tires were recapped and the customer service area, which had a slashed couch, a coffee table with greasy magazines, and an ashtray. He introduced me to Tully, a fat man with one ear, who worked the buffers that resurfaced the white walls. I was handed an apron and a face mask and shown how to use the buffer: Lift the tire and center, inflate it with a footpedal, press the buffer against the white band until cleaned, and then deflate and blow off the tire with an air hose.

With a paint brush he stirred a can of industrial preserver. "Then slap this blue stuff on." While he was talking a co-worker came up quietly from behind him and goosed him with the air hose. Tully jumped as if he had been struck by a bullet and then turned around cussing and cupping his genitals in his hands as the other worker walked away calling out foul names. When Tully turned to me smiling his gray teeth, I lifted my mouth into a smile because I wanted to get along. He has to be on my side, I thought. He's the one who'll tell the foreman how I'm doing.

I worked carefully that day, setting the tires on the machine as if they were babies, since it was easy to catch a finger in the rim that expanded to inflate the tire. At the day's end we swept up the tire dust and emptied the trash into bins.

At five the workers scattered for their cars and motorcycles while I crossed the street to wash at a burger stand. My hair was stiff with dust and my mouth showed pink against the backdrop of my dirty face. I then ordered a hotdog and walked slowly in the direction of the abandoned house where I had stayed the night before. I lay under the trees and within minutes was asleep. When I woke my shoulders were sore and my eyes burned when I squeezed the lids together.

From the backyard I walked dully through a residential street, and as evening came on, the TV glare in the living rooms and the headlights of passing cars showed against the blue drift of dusk. I saw two children coming up the street with snow cones, their tongues darting at the packed ice. I saw a boy with a peach and wanted to stop him, but felt embarrassed by my hunger. I walked for an hour only to return and discover the house lit brightly. Behind the fence I heard voices and saw a flashlight poking at the garage door. A man on the back steps mumbled something about the refrigerator to the one with the flashlight.

I waited for them to leave, but had the feeling they wouldn't because there was the commotion of furniture being moved. Tired, even more desperate, I started walking again with a great urge to kick things and tear the day from my life. I felt weak and my mind kept drifting because of hunger. I crossed the street to a gas station where I sipped at the water fountain and searched the Coke machine for change. I started walking again, first up a commercial street, then into a residential area where I lay down on someone's lawn and replayed a scene at home—my Mother crying at the kitchen table, my stepfather yelling with food in his mouth. They're cruel, I thought, and warned myself that I should never forgive them. How could they do this to me.

When I got up from the lawn it was late. I searched out a place to sleep and found an unlocked car that seemed safe. In the back seat, with my shoes off, I fell asleep but woke up startled about four in the morning when the owner, a nurse on her way to work, opened the door. She got in and was about to start the engine when I raised my head up from the backseat to explain my presence. She screamed so loudly when I said "I'm sorry" that I sprinted from the car with my shoes in hand. Her screams faded, then stopped altogether, as I ran down the block where I hid behind a trash bin and waited for a police siren to sound. Nothing. I crossed the street to a church where I slept stiffly on cardboard in the balcony.

I woke up feeling tired and greasy. It was early and a few street lights were still lit, the east growing pink with dawn. I washed myself from a garden hose and returned to the church to break into what looked like a kitchen. Paper cups, plastic spoons, a coffee pot littered on a table. I found a box of Nabisco crackers which I ate until I was full.

At work I spent the morning at the buffer, but was then told to help Iggy, an old Mexican, who was responsible for choosing tires that could be recapped without the risk of exploding at high speeds. Every morning a truck would deliver used tires, and after I unloaded them Iggy would step among the tires to inspect them for punctures and rips on the side walls.

With a yellow chalk he marked circles and Xs to indicate damage and called out "junk." For those tires that could be recapped, he said "goody" and I placed them on my hand truck.

When I had a stack of eight I kicked the truck at an angle and balanced them to another work area where Iggy again inspected the tires, scratching Xs and calling out "junk."

Iggy worked only until three in the afternoon, at which time he went to the locker room to wash and shave and to dress in a two-piece suit. When he came out he glowed with a bracelet, watch, rings, and a shiny fountain pen in his breast pocket. His shoes sounded against the asphalt. He was the image of a banker stepping into sunlight with millions on his mind. He said a few low words to workers with whom he was friendly and none to people like me.

I was seventeen, stupid because I couldn't figure out the difference between an F 78 14 and 750 14 at sight. Iggy shook his head when I brought him the wrong tires, especially since I had expressed interest in being his understudy. "Mexican, how can you be so stupid?" he would yell at me, slapping a tire from my hands. But within weeks I learned a lot about tires, from sizes and makes to how they are molded in iron forms to how Valley stole from other companies. Now and then we received a truckload of tires, most of them new or nearly new, and they were taken to our warehouse in the back where the serial numbers were ground off with a sander. On those days the foreman handed out Cokes and joked with us as we worked to get the numbers off.

Most of the workers were Mexican or black, though a few redneck whites worked there. The base pay was a dollar sixty-five, but the average was three dollars. Of the black workers, I knew Sugar Daddy the best. His body carried two hundred and fifty pounds, armfuls of scars, and a long knife that made me jump when he brought it out from his boot without warning. At one time he had been a singer, and had cut a record in 1967 called *Love's Chance*, which broke into the R and B charts. But nothing came of it. No big contract, no club dates, no tours. He made very little from the sales, only enough for an operation to pull a steering wheel from his gut when, drunk and mad at a lady friend, he slammed his Mustang into a row of parked cars.

"Touch it," he smiled at me one afternoon as he raised his shirt, his black belly kinked with hair. Scared, I traced the scar that ran from his chest to the left of his belly button, and I was repelled but hid my disgust.

Among the Mexicans I had few friends because I was different, a *pocho* who spoke bad Spanish. At lunch they sat in tires and laughed over burritos, looking up at me to laugh even harder. I also sat in tires while nursing a Coke and felt dirty and sticky because I was still living on the street and had not had a real bath in over a week. Nevertheless, when the border patrol came to round up the nationals, I ran with them as they scrambled for the fence or hid among the tires behind the warehouse. The foreman, who thought I was an undocumented worker, yelled at me to run, to get away. I did just that. At the time it seemed fun because there was no risk, only a goodhearted feeling of hide-and-seek, and besides it meant an hour away from work on company time. When the police left we came back and some of the nationals made up stories of how they were almost caught—how they out-raced the police. Some of the stories were so convoluted and unconvincing that everyone laughed *mentiras*, especially when one described how he overpowered a policeman, took his gun away, and sold the patrol car. We laughed and he laughed, happy to be there to make up a story.

If work was difficult, so were the nights. I still had not gathered enough money to rent a room, so I spent the nights sleeping in parked cars or in the balcony of a church. After a week I found a newspaper ad for room for rent, phoned, and was given directions. Finished with work, I walked the five miles down Mission Road looking back into the traffic with my thumb out. No rides. After eight hours of handling tires I was frightening, I suppose, to drivers since they seldom looked at me; if they did, it was a quick glance. For the next six weeks I would try to hitchhike, but the only person to stop was a Mexican woman who gave me two dollars to take the bus. I told her it was too much and that no bus ran from Mission Road to where I lived, but she insisted that I keep the money and trotted back to her idling car. It must have hurt her to see me day after day walking in the heat and looking very much the dirty Mexican to the many minds that didn't know what it meant to work at hard labor. That woman knew. Her eyes met mine as she opened the car door, and there was a tenderness that was surprisingly true—one for which you wait for years but when it comes it doesn't help. Nothing changes. You continue on in rags, with the sun still above you.

I rented a room from a middle-aged couple whose lives were a mess. She was a school teacher and he was a fireman. A perfect set up, I thought. But during my stay there they would argue with one another for hours in their bedroom.

When I rang at the front door both Mr. and Mrs. Van Deusen answered and didn't bother to disguise their shock at how awful I looked. But they let me in all the same. Mrs. Van Deusen showed me around the house, from the kitchen and bathroom to the living room with its grand piano. On her fingers she counted out the house rules as she walked me to my room. It was a girl's room with lace curtains, scenic wallpaper of a Victorian couple enjoying a stroll, canopied bed, and stuffed animals in a corner. Leaving, she turned and asked if she could do laundry for me and, feeling shy and hurt, I told her no; perhaps the next day. She left and I undressed to take a bath, exhausted as I sat on the edge of the bed probing my aches and my bruised places. With a towel around my waist I hurried down the hallway to the bathroom where Mrs. Van Deusen had set out an additional towel with a tube of shampoo. I ran the water in the tub and sat on the toilet, lid down, watching the steam curl toward the ceiling. When I lowered myself into the tub I felt my body sting. I soaped a wash cloth and scrubbed my arms until they lightened, even glowed pink, but still I looked unwashed around my neck and face no matter how hard I rubbed. Back in the room I sat in bed reading a magazine, happy and thinking of no better luxury than a girl's sheets, especially after nearly two weeks of sleeping on cardboard at the church.

I was too tired to sleep, so I sat at the window watching the neighbors move about in pajamas, and, curious about the room, looked through the bureau drawers to search out personal things—snapshots, a messy diary, and a high school yearbook. I looked up the Van Deusen's daughter, Barbara, and studied her face as if I recognized her from my own school—a face that said "promise," "college," "nice clothes in the closet." She was a skater and a member of the German Club; her greatest ambition was to sing at the Hollywood Bowl.

After awhile I got into bed and as I drifted toward sleep I thought about her. In my mind I played a love scene again and again and altered it slightly each time. She comes home from college and at first is indifferent to my presence in her home, but finally I overwhelm her with deep pity when I come home hurt from work, with blood on my shirt. Then there was another version: Home from college she is immediately taken with me, in spite of my work-darkened face, and invites me into the family car for a milkshake across town. Later, back at the house, we sit in the living room talking about school until we're so close I'm holding her hand. The truth of the matter was that Barbara did come home for a week, but was bitter toward her parents for taking in boarders (two others besides me). During that time she spoke to me only twice: Once, while searching the refrigerator, she asked if we had any mustard; the other time she asked if I had seen her car keys.

But it was a place to stay. Work had become more and more difficult. I not only worked with Iggy, but also with the assistant foreman who was in charge of unloading trucks. After they backed in I hopped on top to pass the tires down by bouncing them on the tailgate to give them an extra spring so they would be less difficult to handle on the other end. Each truck was weighed down with more than two hundred tires, each averaging twenty pounds, so that by the time the truck was emptied and swept clean I glistened with sweat and my T-shirt stuck to my body. I blew snot threaded with tire dust onto the asphalt, indifferent to the customers who watched from the waiting room.

The days were dull. I did what there was to do from morning until the bell sounded at five; I tugged, pulled, and cussed at tires until I was listless and my mind drifted and caught on small things, from cold sodas to shoes to stupid talk about what we would do with a million dollars. I remember unloading a truck with Hamp, a black man.

"What's better than a sharp lady?" he asked me as I stood sweaty on a pile of junked tires. "Water. With ice," I said.

He laughed with his mouth open wide. With his fingers he pinched the sweat from his chin and flicked at me. "You be too young, boy. A woman can make you a god."

As a kid I had chopped cotton and picked grapes, so I knew work. I knew the fatigue and the boredom and the feeling that there was a good possibility you might have to do such work for years, if not for a lifetime. In fact, as a kid I imagined a dark fate: To marry Mexican poor, work Mexican hours, and in the end die a Mexican death, broke and in despair.

But this job at Valley Tire Company confirmed that there was something worse than field work, and I was doing it. We were all doing it, from foreman to the newcomers like me, and what I felt heaving tires for eight hours a day was felt by everyone—black, Mexican, redneck. We all despised those hours but didn't know what else to do. The workers were unskilled, some undocumented and fearful of deportation, and all struck with an uncertainty at what to do with their lives. Although everyone bitched about work, no one left. Some had worked there for as long as twelve years; some had sons working there. Few quit; no one was ever fired. It amazed me that no one gave up when the border patrol jumped from their vans, baton in hand, because I couldn't imagine any work that could be worse—or any life. What was out there, in the world, that made men run for the fence in fear?

Iggy was the only worker who seemed sure of himself. After five hours of "junking," he brushed himself off, cleaned up in the washroom, and came out gleaming with an elegance that humbled the rest of us. Few would look him straight in the eye or talk to him in our usual stupid way because he was so much better. He carried himself as a man should—with that old world "dignity"—while the rest of us muffed our jobs and talked dully about dull things as we worked. From where he worked in his open shed he would now and then watch us with his hands on his hips. He would shake his head and click his tongue in disgust.

The rest of us lived dismally. I often wondered what the others' homes were like; I couldn't imagine that they were much better than our work place. No one indicated that his outside life was interesting or intriguing. We all looked defeated and contemptible in our filth at the day's end. I imagined the average welcome at home: Rafael, a Mexican national who had worked at Valley for five years, returned to a beaten house of kids who were dressed in mismatched clothes and playing kick-the-can. As for Sugar Daddy, he returned home to a stuffy room where he would read and reread old magazines. He ate potato chips, drank beer, and watched TV. There was no grace in dipping socks into a wash basin where later he would wash his cup and plate.

There was no grace at work. It was all ridicule. The assistant foreman drank Cokes in front of the newcomers as they laced tires in the afternoon sun. Knowing that I had a long walk home,

Rudy, the college student, passed me waving and yelling "Hello," as I started down Mission Road on the way home to eat out of cans. Even our plump secretary got into the act by wearing short skirts and flaunting her milky legs. If there was love, it was ugly. I'm thinking of Tully and an older man whose name I can no longer recall fondling one another in the washroom. I had come in cradling a smashed finger to find them pressed together in the shower, their pants undone and partly pulled down. When they saw me they smiled their pink mouths but didn't bother to push away.

How we arrived at such a place is a mystery to me. Why anyone would stay for years is even a deeper concern. You showed up, but from where? What broken life? What ugly past? The foreman showed you the Coke machine, the washroom, and the yard where you'd work. When you picked up a tire, you were amazed at the black it could give off.

Being Stupid

What evilness had risen from my hand? Once, when I and a neighbor friend, Rinehart, a true Okie and lover of gravy on cantaloupe, were on the front porch, a very drunk man in a brown overcoat staggered down our street in the middle of the afternoon. He reeled like those drunks in the afternoon movies—side to side, forward and then backward, all the while slurring words at himself and things that got in his way.

Rinehart and I watched him pass, thinking it was funny that he should have to lean against a car and hold on. Then the brilliant idea: Why not sell him a beer bottle filled with water? We beamed at each other and rushed off to find a bottle before the drunk escaped our scheme. Pulling one from the garbage, we filled it with water from the garden hose and then ran after the drunk who had not wandered too far. Rinehart was standing behind me, somewhat scared, when I yelled: "Mister, you wanna buy a beer? Look at this." I held up the bottle like a chalice and pointed at it. He turned slowly to show us his watery eyes. His stare drifted, and out came: "Whaaaat?" It was an ugly sound that scared both of us. Still, when the drunk took a dollar from his pocket, I snatched it from him and then set the bottle at his feet. He tried to lunge at me, but I sidestepped him and he fell to the ground, tipping over the bottle. He looked at the bottle, then back at me, and whined from some terrible cavity of the heart: "You'll get yours, sonny." The words scared me. I was Catholic. I knew right from wrong and what he meant.

The drunk rose to his feet with difficulty and then bent down to pick up the beer bottle and raise it to his mouth. As he continued down the street, we watched in silence as he crossed the street into the next block. I turned to Rinehart and tried to be funny by crossing my eyes but his face had gone slack from bad feelings. I suggested that we cash the dollar, but he didn't want anything to do with it. He left me and went inside. What could I do? What was done was done. With the dollar I bought a Coke, potato chips, and a lemon pie, and rode my bike up and down the block, now and then staring at Rinehart's house and feeling bad.

I marched through life in evilness, and perhaps a low point that will surely send me tumbling into hell was when Scott, my best friend and still another lover of cantaloupe and gravy, begged me to break into his sister's house with him. She was on vacation in Yosemite, so it was a perfect time to undo a window screen, slither through, and come out smiling with the stereo, the color TV, the alarm clock, the antique silver, or whatever our hearts desired.

"Come on, Gar, no way are we gonna get caught," he beat over my head all night. "We could put the stereo in the closet, and sell the rest of the stuff. Fifty-fifty."

At first I was surprised at Scott. My mouth hung open, and when I closed it it fell open again. His own sister's house? His recently married sister? I would never have thought of stealing from family or, for that matter, stealing period. I was Catholic. I believed in evilness.

But then, Scott's arguments sort of made sense. Didn't we in fact need a stereo and wasn't it true that we were stealing from the rich? Surely no harm would result. His sister worked for the government and his brother-in-law was employed as a surveyor. He made a killing, we thought, and there were benefits to boot.

"Gar, we could do it. No one will know," he argued for hours before I finally came around to agree with him. We planned our break-in for the following night, and then sat back in our beds bragging about what we would buy: Vienna sausages, cheeses, and assorted packages of Lipton soup, our favorite. Our imaginations narrowed to Cokes, Cheez-its, and puffed bags of Cheetos. Okie Heaven, we laughed.

Our circumstances were laughable. Mad at my parents, I had said "shit" under my breath and had joined Scott in renting a small room in a boarding house. We each had a bed, a chair, and one wobbly table where we fixed our meals. We lived like monks with bad eating habits: For breakfast there were Froot Loops and Sonny Boy orange juice; for lunch we slurped up a bowl of Lipton soup, along with a thin sandwich of peanut butter and jelly; for dinner, which I ate alone because Scott worked the night shift at a box factory, I often opened a can of Campbell's Manhandler. Great stuff, I thought at the time—a time when I was trying to become a poet. I had taped my poems (all three of them) to the wall near the window where I ate, re-reading them as I weighed each steaming spoonful of my Manhandler. When a breeze came in the poems fluttered and hung on the verge of pulling off the wall and coming alive. Good stuff, I thought, but the professor I would show them to that fall would think different. The poems died in his class, or limped like old dogs in the hallway, and when I tried to tape them back to the wall they slipped behind the bed where I left them, depressed.

Scott worked hard hours while I lived on social security. Ninety dollars every month. Thirty dollars for rent, twenty for food, and fifteen for gas. There were other expenses that might have amounted to five dollars, but I managed to save the rest for a rainy day.

But it was the end of a lean month, so we agreed to rob the house. The next night Scott called in sick and as we were about to leave, a friend of ours showed up. It was Ronnie in a baseball cap; Ronnie the biologist in lime green socks; the big creep who squeezed pimples at mirrors and laughed.

"Where you guys going?" he asked. "For a walk," I lied. He followed us downstairs and the three of us walked one block, then another, and then still another. We returned to the house and at that point we told Ronnie what we were going to do. His face was like an orange moon when he asked if he could come along. We shouted no and then told him to get lost. And that's just what he did. He got into his '57 Chevy, a car only a Mexican or a redneck looks good in. Ronnie was neither.

Scott and I jumped into my '49 Plymouth and raced to Scott's sister's place. By the time we got there Ronnie was waiting for us on his car hood with his long legs dangling and his socks showing under a street light. He called to us, and we shushed him.

"OK, you can come with us," Scott told him, "but don't be

too greedy. Just take what you really need." Scott explained to us that he would climb through the upstairs window that he knew was open. I drove my Plymouth into the alley behind the house; Ronnie parked his Chevy on the end of the block. By the time Ronnie and I returned to the house, we could make out Scott's crouched figure waving for us to come in. We tiptoed past the spray of car parts and gardening tools, up the back porch, and into the house. In the kitchen Scott again warned us, Ronnie in particular, just to take things that we needed. He flicked on the flashlight and Scott and I went to the living room while Ronnie, who was offended by Scott's warnings, went upstairs to search the bedrooms. A match lit the way for him.

Scott and I unplugged the stereo and detached the speaker wires from the receiver. I cradled the speakers one at a time, like babies, to the alley while Scott propped the receiver and turntable on his shoulders and followed me. Together we carried the 19-inch RCA, dropping it once on the lawn and again in the alley when we tried to fit it into the trunk. When the neighbor's dog snorted at the fence, we froze and tried not to breathe.

Meanwhile, Ronnie had brought down a tape recorder, some record albums, and a hat. "Don't be stupid," I told him in a low but angry voice. I slapped the hat from his hand and he said, "Oh."

The three of us returned to the house where we searched for small things: Fountain pens, loose change, a wad of bills sandwiched under a mattress. Scott's flashlight poked at the dark, and I followed it, looking desperately for something—anything—of value. Ronnie started upstairs to search the bedrooms again when we heard a car coming to a stop. The neighbors. We grew still and listened to the car door slam, a low voice, and then a hee-haw of laughter as they climbed their steps. This frightened me and Scott, but Ronnie remained indifferent. "Don't worry."

But we did. I could feel that Scott was scared out of his wits, so I told him to stay calm while I took one last look around the house. It was then that I found a plexiglas bank of quarters, dimes and nickels. I weighed it in my palm: At least twenty dollars, I thought.

When I returned to the living room Scott was peeking out the window. He turned to me and his voice was full of panic.

"C'mon, let's get outta here."

At the stairs I called up to Ronnie to come down, but, a true fool to the bone, he said no. I climbed the stairs where I found him in a closet searching on his knees among the shoes. I grabbed him by the arm, but he tugged away.

"You'll get it later, punk," I told him. My mouth was puckered with meanness and instead of waiting for later I jumped into the closet to fight him. Scott came running up the stairs to break us up. When I got up my lip felt warm and my back hurt where Ronnie had pounded me with a high-heeled shoe.

"Let's go, Ronnie," Scott begged, but still he refused to leave. "Listen, just give me some more time. Just ten more minutes."

We went downstairs without him and into the alley where we placed the stereo in the back seat of the car, jumped in, and began to drive slowly down the alley. A large branch, somehow stuck to the underbody of the car, scraped against the ground and got louder as we picked up speed. The neighborhood of dogs whined, then broke the night with barks, as a porch light came one. Out of the alley I drove madly hoping the branch would snap. But it didn't. We drove all the way home with the branch screeching and in my mind I prayed to God and confessed our evilness. "Baby Jesus, get us out of here. Save our asses."

Back at our room we sat on our beds trying to figure out the next move. Where would we sell the stereo? Sunnyside Swapmeet? Cherry Auction? Should we drag the stuff into our room? What if anyone saw us? We went round and round fluttering with fear like chickens. Scott paced the room, searching out the window now and then, while I lay on the bed, exhausted.

Then we made out the sound of Ronnie's car in the distance. It got louder and his tires skidded when he turned the corner to our block. He stopped with the screech of bad brakes, revved up the engine, and then shut it off. He got out of his car and I could hear the flipflop of K-mart sneakers climb our stairs. When I opened the door for him he was holding a lamp with a torn shade. I couldn't believe it. What had gotten into his mind to make him bring back a lamp?

Immediately we began to argue. I pushed him; he pushed me. I pushed him again and we started fighting, our arms flailing at one another as we banged against the table and the bed. Scott sat on his bed with his head in his hands and suffered in private shame, indifferent to our rolling about the room. A banging came from the wall, followed by a "Shut up in there." Ronnie and I let go of each other and got up breathing hard and pressing at the hurt places throbbing under the skin. I looked into the mirror that showed a long scratch from Ronnie's girlish fingernails. *Scarface Soto.*

Ronnie dabbed at a bloody tooth with a napkin and gave me a dirty look. He looked in the mirror, his index fingers stretching his mouth open to show a yellow tongue.

The three of us then collapsed on the beds, with Scott and I in one and Ronnie lying face down in the other. Minutes later Ronnie got up, picked up his lamp, and left without saying a word. I got up and watched from the window as Ronnie roared off in his Chevy. I turned to Scott whose face was buried in the pillow. When I called to him he let out his fear: "Oh, man, are we in trouble."

He got up quickly and looked at me. "Gar, we're going to leave town. That's the only way. We'll say that we were out of town. San Francisco. My brother lives there."

We went on building an alibi as he changed his socks, readying for the bus ride up north. We got our toothbrushes, a change of clothes, and fixed sandwiches: Six of them slapped together with tuna and limp sheets of lettuce. We hurried into the car and drove off in silence, each of us gnawed by shame and fear. Why had we done it? Didn't we come from OK families? What drug had forced Scott to propose such deceit? It was the only time I had stolen, and guilt clamped my head like a football helmet.

Instead of going straight to the Greyhound Bus depot, we stopped at Ronnie's apartment where we found him face down in a pillow. Incense burned in an ashtray on a nightstand, a thread of smoke unraveling. The lamp leaned like a rifle against the bed.

"Leave me alone," he moaned without looking up. I threw myself into a chair and Scott coaxed him to come to San Francisco with us.

"You gotta come, man," Scott whined. His hands were cocked on his hips. "Get your face up and let's go. Now, *menso.*"

Ronnie moaned into his pillow, "Leave me alone."

Scott and I left and drove near the bus terminal, where we

parked on an unlit street with no meters. The "stuff" was still in the back seat, and this made us feel uneasy. What if the car were towed? For sure the cops would trace the TV and stereo, we thought. We sat in the car ripping up our fingernails with our teeth and thought deeply before we started off in the direction of the terminal, past a few winos who mumbled at us like drunk priests.

At the terminal we stood in a line of greasy people who were, in my imagination, fleeing from their own predicaments. What crimes had they committed? Burglary? Forged checks? Severe knife wounds? I studied their broken faces and the clipclop of their limps. I watched them play the pinball machines and slouch at the quarter-for-a-half-hour TV sets. Some sat in plastic orange chairs while others smoked and leaned on the wall with Cokes in their hands.

I searched the terminal and everyone looked scuffed up or worn to the bone, especially the ones in mismatched clothes: Flowered shirts with striped pants.

When the man behind the counter said six dollars and seventy-five cents to San Francisco, I searched Scott's face and he stared back because we didn't have more than twenty dollars between us. Still, we paid and waited in another line that was slowly gobbled by the door. We passed through as the bus driver punched hungrily at our tickets. He pointed to a bus and we boarded, sitting stiffly as cardboard in cushioned seats.

I turned to Scott who was trembling and working on his fingernails again. "Do you think we're doing the right thing? I mean, we only got about five bucks."

He turned to me. His face was pale despite the dark stubble that rose like iron filings from his chin. "Let's get outta here."

Rising from my seat I pulled our six-sandwich lunch from the rack above our heads. Outside, Scott explained to the bus driver that we had forgotten our wallets at home; we couldn't possibly make the trip.

"Now why the hell didn't you think about that before you bought tickets," he asked in a gruff voice. He shook his head and slurred: "Jesus Christ."

We looked down at our shoes, then away, as the driver wrote something on our tickets. "Now go on," he waved. "Jesus Christ."

We stood in line again, but I noticed that the people who were milling around didn't look all that bad after all. Perhaps I had been hasty in my observations, a college snot. I again noted the man in the flowered shirt with the striped pants and he didn't look so bad. He was probably a homeowner, a two-car man with a Catholic background, a league bowler.

After a few minutes of arguing our case, we were refunded our money and dashed from the terminal into the night to jog up Tulare Street back to the car. We leaned against the fender, bent over with our hands on our knees to catch our breath.

"We've got to straighten up," I told Scott, remorseful at our stupidity.

Scott, who had been locked in thought, proposed that we return the stuff; that the only way out was to get rid of it because he was certain that his family would find out, if not in the coming week, then in a month or a year. His sister might show up at our hovel and, with our luck, the stereo would be blaring with The Stones and the TV glowing blue with the sound turned down.

We threw this idea back and forth like a football. It was in my hands when we agreed that the stuff had to go back.

We drove back to Ronnie's place where he was still face down in the pillow. When Scott called to him, he moaned, "Leave me alone. We're fools." He threw his head back into the pillow. "Fools."

"Listen, *menso*, we gotta do something about this stuff," I told him. I took a sandwich from our bag and tossed one to Scott who tossed it back to me. "I ain't hungry."

I unwrapped the sandwich and listened to Scott explain to Ronnie our plan of returning the television and stereo and the rest of the stuff. Ronnie listened with his eyes closed while rolling his tongue over God knows what filth in his mouth. He rose up on his elbow and blinked his red eyes at us. "Fools!"

I threw the tuna sandwich at him and again reminded him that when it was all over, I was going to ride a bike up his back, make him hurt.

"Let's go," I told Scott. I picked up the lamp that Ronnie had taken and propped it on my shoulder. From there we drove to Scott's sister's place where we parked in the alley. For a few minutes we sat in silence, each of us mulling over in private our fears. The night was busy with crickets, a whole tribe I imagined, but when we got out they stopped. Everything was still. I was amazed at the clarity of the moon that had just cleared the telephone wires toward a new day. In the distance a dog started to bark, followed by another, and then still another. We leaned against the car and waited for them to stop their racket. When they did, Scott turned to me. "I'll go first. Wait for me."

He pressed the flashlight against his palm: It showed blood red. He walked away and I sat on the car hood to warm myself against the late night chill. I thought of how stupid we had been. Of all people we stole from a relative. A sister. A recently married sister. I said a made-up prayer and assured God that if I got out of this one I'd be good. No problems from me—ever!

Scott returned to the car to help me lift the television that we carried solemnly like a coffin through the yard into the house. We set it on its side in the kitchen and returned to the car for the stereo, the alarm clock, the lamp, and the small things. We set them in the kitchen and rested there for a moment, our breathing like a saw going through wood, before we returned to the car. We drove home sweating but relieved, and instead of going inside we sat in the car wondering if we would be found out. Fingerprints? A dropped pencil with my teethmarks for the crime lab to work from? Anything was possible.

We sat in the dark, pensive but limp from the exertion of fear, and stared ahead up the street, mumbling the different versions of our crime. A dog crossed the street. A collie. What a lucky life, I thought, to chow down a bowl of Skippy dog food and trot off for an eventful night of dog fights and knocked-over garbage cans. What freedom from conscience. When we were kids of thirteen and fourteen we had done the same: Downed a bowl of Frosted Flakes and then met somewhere, in a vacant lot or a corner, to begin a day of wandering through the streets of Fresno in search of trouble. There had been no better time.

The dog trotted in our direction. Rolling down my window I called to him: "Come here, boy." He stopped still, his head poised beautifully under the street light, before he started to wag his tail. He came up to the car, almost shyly, and I let my hand hang from the window. He licked it and made a whining noise. I opened the door to the back seat and the dog climbed in, his tail patting the upholstery as he whined to be scratched and loved.

Unwrapping a tuna sandwich, I poked it at the dog's nose and he nibbled at it with more manners than most people I knew.

Scott was still lost in the vacancy of his own private guilt, so when I asked him if he wanted to go to Sambo's for breakfast because I knew we couldn't sleep that night, he mumbled, "Yeah, maybe, why not." Scott gnawed a fingernail of shame, and I figured a good stack of pancakes would do wonders.

I turned to the collie. "What do you think, baby?" The dog whined and pumped its tiny feet which made me love it. I started the engine, put it in gear, and started up the street while the dog's head hung over the front seat and washed the backs of my ears.

The Savings Book

My wife, Carolyn, married me for my savings: Not the double digit figures but the strange three or four dollar withdrawals and deposits. The first time she saw my passbook she laughed until her eyes became moist and then hugged me as she called "Poor baby." And there was truth to what she was saying: Poor.

I remember opening my savings account at Guarantee Savings May 27, 1969, which was a Monday. The previous Saturday my brother and I had taken a labor bus to chop cotton in the fields west of Fresno. We returned home in the back of a pickup with fourteen dollars each and a Mexican national who kept showing us watches and rings for us to buy. That day my brother and I wouldn't spring for Cokes or sandwiches, as most eveyone else on our crew did when a vending truck drove up at lunch time, tooting a loud horn. The driver opened the aluminum doors to display his goods, and the workers, who knew better but couldn't resist, hovered over the iced Cokes, the cellophaned sandwiches, and the Hostess cupcakes. We looked on from the shade of the bus, sullen and most certainly sensible. Why pay forty cents when you could get a Coke in town for half the price. Why buy a sandwich for sixty-five cents when you could have slapped together your own sandwich. That was what our mother had done for us. She had made us tuna sandwiches which by noon had grown suspiciously sour when we peeled back the top slice to peek in. Still, we ate them, chewing slowly and watching each other to see if he were beginning to double over. Finished, we searched the paper bag and found a broken stack of saltine crackers wrapped in wax paper. What a cruel mother, we thought. Dry crackers on a dry day when it was sure to rise into the nineties as we chopped cotton or, as the saying went, "played Mexican golf."

We had each earned fourteen dollars for eight hours of work, the most money I had ever made in one day. Two days later, on May 27, 1969, I deposited those dollars; on June 9th I made my first withdrawal—four dollars to buy a belt to match a pair of pants. I had just been hired to sell encyclopedias, and the belt was intended to dazzle my prospective clients when they opened the door to receive me. But in reality few welcomed my presence on their doorsteps and the only encyclopedias I sold that summer were to families on welfare who so desperately wanted to rise from their soiled lives. Buy a set, I told them, and your problems will disappear. Knowledge is power. Education is the key to the future, and so on. The contracts, however, were rescinded and my commissions with them.

On June 20 I withdrew three dollars and twenty-five cents to buy a plain white shirt because my boss had suggested that I should look more "professional." Still, I sold encyclopedias to the poor and again the contracts were thrown out. Finally I was fired, my briefcase taken away, and the company tie undone from my neck. I walked home in the summer heat despairing at the consequence: No new clothes for the fall.

On July 13 I took out five dollars and eighty cents which, including the five cents interest earned, left me with a balance of one dollar. I used the money for bus fare to Los Angeles to look for work. I found it in a tire factory. At summer's end I returned home and walked proudly to Guarantee Savings with my pockets stuffed with ten dollar bills. That was September 5, and my new balance jumped to one hundred and forty-one dollars. I was a senior in high school and any withdrawals from my account went exclusively to buy clothes, never for food, record albums, or concerts. On September 15, for instance, I withdrew fifteen dollars for a shirt and jeans. On September 24 I again stood before the teller to ask for six dollars. I bought a sweater at the Varsity Shop at Coffee's.

Slowly my savings dwindled that fall semester, although I did beef it up with small deposits: Twenty dollars on October 1, ten dollars on November 19, fifteen dollars on December 31, and so on. But by February my savings account balance read three

The Savings Book 135

dollars and twelve cents. On March 2 I returned to the bank to withdraw one crisp dollar to do God knows what. Perhaps it was to buy my mother a birthday gift. Seven days later, on March 10, I made one last attempt to bolster my savings by adding eight dollars. By March 23, however, I was again down to one dollar.

By the time I finally closed my account, it had fluctuated for five years, rising and falling as a barometer to my financial quandry. What is curious to me about this personal history are the kinds of transactions that took place—one day I would withdraw three dollars while on another day I would ask for six. How did it vanish? What did it buy? I'm almost certain I bought clothes but for what occasion? For whom? I didn't have a girlfriend in my senior year, so where did the money go?

To withdraw those minor amounts was no easy task. I had to walk or bicycle nearly four miles, my good friend Scott tagging along, and afterward we'd walk up and down the Fresno Mall in search of the elusive girlfriend or, if worse came to worst, to look for trouble.

My savings book is a testimony to my fear of poverty—that by saving a dollar here, another there, it would be kept at bay.

I admit that as a kid I worried about starving, although there was probably no reason. There was always something to eat; the cupboards were weighed down with boxes of this and that. But when I was older the remembrance of difficult times stayed with me: The time Mother was picking grapes and my brother ate our entire lunch while my sister and I played under the vines. For us there was nothing to eat that day. The time I opened the refrigerator at my father's (who was separated from our mother at the time) to stare at one puckered apple that sat in the conspicuous glare of the refrigerator's light. I recalled my uncle lying on a couch dying of cancer. I recalled my father who died from an accident a year later and left us in even more roughed up shoes. I had not been born to be scared out of my wits, but that is what happened. Through a set of experiences early in my life, I grew up fearful that some financial tragedy would strike at any moment, as when I was certain that the recession of 1973 would lead to chaos—burned cars and street fighting. During the recession I roomed with my brother and I suggested that we try to become vegetarians. My brother looked up from his drawing board and replied: "Aren't we already?" I thought about it for a while, and it was true. I was getting most of my hearty meals from my girlfriend, Carolyn, who would later become my wife. She had a job with great pay, and when she opened her refrigerator I almost wept for the bologna, sliced ham, and drumsticks. I spied the cheeses and imported olives, tomatoes, and the artichoke hearts. I opened the freezer—chocolate ice cream!

At that time Carolyn put up with my antics, so when I suggested that we buy fifty dollars worth of peanut butter and pinto beans to store under her bed, she happily wrote out a check because she was in love and didn't know any better. I was certain that in 1974 the country would slide into a depression and those who were not prepared would be lost. We hid the rations in the house and sat at the front window to wait for something to happen.

What happened was that we married and I loosened up. I still fear the worst, but the worst is not what it once was. Today I bought a pair of shoes; tomorrow I may splurge to see a movie, with a box of popcorn and a large soda that will wash it all down. It's time to live, I tell myself, and if a five dollar bill flutters from my hands, no harm will result. I laugh at the funny scenes that aren't funny, and I can't think of any better life.

	DATE	WITHDRAWALS	INTEREST	ADDITIONS	BALANCE	SYM.
1	MAY 27			14.00	14.00	
2	JUN -9	4.00			10.00	
3	JUN 20	3.25			6.75	
4	JUL-1		.05		6.80	
5	JUL-1	5.80			1.00	
6	SEP -5			140.00	141.00	
7	SEP 17	15.00			126.00	
8	SEP 24	6.00			120.00	
9	OCT -8	QUARTERLY INTEREST	.55		120.55	
10	OCT -8	20.00			100.55	
11	OCT 16	20.00			80.55	
12	NOV 28	10.55			70.00	

FRESNO GUARANTEE

SAVINGS AND LOAN ASSOCIATION

	DATE	WITHDRAWALS	INTEREST	ADDITIONS	BALANCE	SYM.
13	DEC 11	10.00			60.00	
14	DEC 22	4.00			56.00	
15	DEC 29		1.00		57.00	
16	DEC 29	22.00			35.00	
17	JAN 19	6.00			29.00	
18	FEB 12	4.00			25.00	
19	FEB 26	8.00			17.00	
20	MAR -5	7.00			10.00	
21	MAR 23	9.00			1.00	
22	MAY -1			50.00	51.00	
23	MAY -1		.28		51.28	
24	JUN -5	6.28			45.00	

SAFETY OF YOUR SAVINGS INSURED
UP TO $15,000 BY FEDERAL SAVINGS
AND LOAN INSURANCE CORPORATION

Getting By

What was there to do in summer? After seeing my wife off to work at 7:00 in the morning, I climbed back into bed and fell asleep with our cat Benny, who was equally oblivious to the fact that most people were off to their tasks of making money. I slept hard, open-mouthed and dreaming and woke up about ten to a spear of sunlight through the curtained window—a window that was screenless so that a few flies, loosened from tuna cans and pie tins in the alley, circled the room, their blue engines coming and going from the window to the different points of my body.

It was mid-morning—or two-and-a-half hours after my wife had started answering questions about financial aid at Fresno State—when I sat at the kitchen table with my coffee and the *Fresno Bee* opened first to baseball scores, then to the tragic murders or attempted murders, then back to baseball scores. The facts always woke me up.

By eleven I was dressed in jeans and a comfortably loose T-shirt. I sat in the living room, legs crossed, and literally waited for a poem to surface from a brain cell, because I was clear-headed and eager to push words from one side of the page to the next. I was eager to reinvent my childhood, to show others the chinaberry tree, ants, shadows, dirty spoons—those nouns that made up much of my poetry. On that day in August nothing came except a few stilted lines about loneliness in contemporary society. I felt sick. The poems I had written in the previous weeks had been dismal efforts to rekindle a feel for the past. There I was, author of a prize-winning collection of poems, with another on the way, and I was troubled, even scared, that an empty head might weigh my previously square and confident shoulders. I sipped another coffee and rechecked the murders, this time in the *Fresno Guide*, and still came up with "loneliness in contemporary society."

We lived in a complex of seven identical cottages which, if in another part of town, might have been considered charming and even historically interesting. But our complex sat between busy streets in an area of loud service vehicles. We were fenced in on three sides by Barnett's Key Shop, a bar called The Space, and an adult movie house called The Venus. It was a "convenient" area. If one day I had locked myself out of our cottage, I could have shouted and Mr. Barnett would have heard; if I had grumbled at my bad luck, I could have downed beers at The Space and talked with those who couldn't talk and felt much better about myself; or if I had lusted over the unattainably wicked, I could have crossed the street and entered the cool dark of The Venus to sit among the fidgeting patrons, their laps full of popcorn.

Because the area was suspiciously run-down, the rent was only a hundred dollars. We were in the seventh cottage, some distance from the busy streets and milky stares of the regulars leaving The Space. It was a relatively quiet complex since most tenants were retired. One of them was a slow-shuffling problem-drinker named Ziggy. His problem was that he couldn't get enough. By late morning, after making a few swipes at the sidewalk with a broom and stooping for candy wrappers that had scuttled in from the rush of traffic, he was ready to put on a jacket and take the 50 or so steps to The Space where he spent the day mumbling, head down and looking into beers. Like most quiet alcoholics, Ziggy was common and uninteresting, except that he had become friend to cockroaches. "Those critters ain't nothin'...thur like you and me," he said to me once at his front door and waved for me to come with him. I followed lamely and was led in shuffles to his kitchen. When the light went on, hundreds of cockroaches began to scatter and bump into one another, creating a dull clicking sound. Ziggy laughed stupidly and watched my face wrinkle with a frown as I stepped back, obviously disgusted. In a way this was Ziggy's entertainment: To lure a person to his cottage in order to laugh at a startled face when the lights went on and the floor began to move.

The other tenants kept to themselves, and we did the same. That summer we poked a few holes in the triangle-shaped plot behind the cottage and planted zucchini and tomatoes. Within a month the zucchini fattened and the tomatoes were bloated red as Christmas ornaments. In the evening I often sat behind the cottage marveling at how these plants had grown scraggly with fruit; how from small plugs they had taken over the small patch of earth within a matter of weeks, inviting snails, worms, spiders, and "creepy things" I couldn't even begin to name. I considered anything that didn't talk, bark, meow, roar, screech, chirp, or hee-haw an insect. It made the world much easier to understand.

By late July we were eating tomatoes daily: Eggs and tomatoes for breakfast, tomatoes bleeding between two slices of toast for lunch, and tomatoes in an austere salad of lettuce and vinegar for dinner. A late evening snack might be a chilled tomato enjoyed in front of Johnny Carson when the air conditioner had just been turned off and the windows raised, the night heat slowly descending upon us like a heavy jacket.

By early August we were at the point of unloading bags of tomatoes and zucchini onto our relatives who, in turn, wanted to shove even larger bags of the same into our arms. Throughout Fresno the gardens were full and a whole community busied itself trying to force gifts of home grown produce on one another. "Here, let's look at photos of our vacation, and while we're at it, let me give you a couple of bags of zucchini," one might say to a favorite uncle, the garden at home producing more than one could possibly pass around on a good evening.

It had been a difficult year for my wife and me. We had returned in May from Mexico City with little money to inherit this cottage from my brother who was on the way up to an apartment with beamed ceilings and a swimming pool. He had had enough of the drunks who seemed forever circling the cottages, on occasion knocking at his door to borrow a wrench to fix their steaming cars or to use the telephone because they were bleeding under their shirts.

We gladly moved in. We painted one room, then another. We became ambitious and waxed the hardwood floors with my worst T-shirts. We tore off the contact paper stuck on the bathroom window, fitting it with a bright yellow shade. A week later the apartment was in order, and the next order of business was to find jobs. We scanned the want ads; we thumbed through the job listings at the unemployment building and followed the faintest rumor of work. But the truth was that neither of us wanted to be locked into jobs. We therefore brainstormed to figure a way to get by without going outside the house and came up with sign painting. An artist by training, Carolyn could paint FM Motors, A-1 Body Shop, Victor's Repo Depot and the like with little effort. This decided, I was made salesman and my first attempt was to snare Garoupa's Grocery, which had just moved next to The Space. A mistake for the owner, but money for us we thought.

Garoupa, a second-generation Portuguese whose laughter rose from his belly first and then into his mouth, was a small-time capitalist. He had come to love money late in his life and worked eagerly at becoming successful, first with a small store that was no bigger than a child's bedroom and then a full-fledged grocery with a meat counter and vegetable bins—what zucchini could not be given away wound up in his grocery slowly growing soft.

"Go out there and do it," Carolyn said. I put on an ironed shirt, slipped into my best shoes and walked to his front door briskly with a sense of audacity. But when I opened the screened door, I spotted Garoupa behind the meat counter sniffing a handful of ground round. He threw it back into the glassed counter and asked if I needed help. I looked around, from the smoke-dusted ceiling to the poorly stocked shelves. A flurry of small fans stirred the air, and I, with cold feet, pretended not to hear him and went off to search the vegetable bins. Yes, the zucchini was there, puckering in the heat. I picked one up, weighed it, and tapped it in my palm, a maneuver that gave me time to muster courage. I didn't know how to approach this burly character. What words could I use to ask for work. "Hey there, Big Daddy, how 'bout me painting a sign for you," I could say to which he might wave, "Get outta here." There I was, a prize-winning poet, with another book on the way, growing useless before bins of sad vegetables. I knew the works of the best poets of this century, most of the novelists, and the short story writer who wrote: "There's every reason to cry." I had studied the Bible. I had underlined passages from Hamlet and knew an epigram from the Vietnamese by heart: "Spit straight up and learn something," which I easily could have applied to that day.

I examined an onion, then a handful of limp peas, and then turned to Garoupa. I searched his coughing face behind the meat counter, a face the color of the sausage he was selling. He wiped his mouth slowly and said: "Yes!" I asked for raisins to which he replied he had none. I turned to the freezer and bought a Popsicle and brought it home to Carolyn. It was her favorite: Cherry. I broke it in two, and it was something like love, the juice running down our arms.

Garoupa's Grocery started slowly but later snowballed into a success. He himself became adventurous and opened Garoupa's Dance Studio next to The Venus. I suppose he imagined that after watching a porno flick patrons might want to rush next door to take lessons in the Cha-Cha. Perhaps so. The dance studio, too, became a success, but later closed for reasons we were not much interested in; we were gone and living in the Bay Area.

Carolyn found a job in financial aid at Fresno State and I was left to my own devices: reading Yourcenar's *Hadrian's Memoirs* and writing poems that I crushed into balls and hurled at our cat Benny. The poems failed to excite, although when Carolyn came home, red and steaming from the ten mile drive from work, I hugged and kissed and told her about the wonderfully effortless lines that I had written for the day—lines that would raise us from our poverty. "I'm boy wonder," I often told her, flexing my muscles. She would go through a pantomime of excitement and rub them, cooing: "O you hot Latins."

When it was obvious that, for whatever reason, the poems I had been writing were bad, I began to consider finding a real job. Gas station attendant, car salesman, apprentice baker? The choices were endlessly sad, and so was I when I woke one day to the realization that I could only write and teach poetry and grow sad after each chapter of *Madame Bovary*. I thought of my brother who, at twenty-two and down to three dollars and an ashtray of pennies, said "Damn," pumped up the tires of my old bike and rode off to the Whirl Wind Car Wash to plead for work—my brother the artist, the not-so-hot guitar player, child of a difficult past.

So this is what it's like, I thought as I scanned the want ads in the *Fresno Bee*, scratching out the god-awful jobs, which left mostly technical ones—dental hygienist or landscape architect— or those that rang suspiciously false: Earn money at home...I spotted, however a promising lead:

Summer Help Needed
Pacific Telephone Company
800 N. Fulton, East Side
An Equal Opportunity Employer

and suddenly I grew confident that things would work; that my application would be admired—the education, the teaching experience, the world travel—and passed to the higher ups who, in turn, would beam, "That's our man!"

I called Jon Veinberg, who had been my roommate in graduate school and my best man at our wedding, and the next morning, just after eight, he came riding up on his bicycle, already sweating from the Fresno heat which had been balancing between 103 and 104 for the past few days. We had iced tea on the front porch and talked poetry: Montale and Hikmet, Transtromer and Stern.

At nine we got up stiffly from the porch, slightly reluctant about following through with our plans, and began the three-block walk down the alley (yet another landmark of this cluster of cottages) to the telephone company. When we arrived a staggered line was forming, and we linked ourselves to it, waving at a few friends we recognized, one of whom was an artist—and a very good one! We joked about "selling out," but secretly we were all hoping for the best.

Within fifteen minutes we were inside sitting on folding chairs and filling out a simple application. One set of questions asked: Last Job? How Many Hours per Week? I wrote T.A. in English and three hours. I smiled at this fact and shared it with Jon who chuckled behind his moustache—a great wirey moustache that nearly touched his collar bones when he was sitting down. "You lie, sucker," he said. "You only worked two." We laughed into each other's faces and returned the applications to the would-be interviewer. Instead of returning to my seat I circled the room studying the equally unemployable who were dressed in faded jeans, T-shirts, mismatched leisure suits, baseball caps, pointlessly loud shoes, rubber thongs—the unemployable in long hair or cropped hair, their cigarettes rolled in the sleeves of their T-shirts. I spotted one face in particular, a Chicano I recognized from high school, and walked over to say *Orale ese!* We shook hands, raza style, and passed stories back and forth like a beach ball: Our marriages, children, cars, and misplaced friends.

I wished him luck and went to sit with Jon. He too was studying the people because his face looked defeated. He stared at me and I at him, and no words were necessary to say times were bad.

I perked up, however, when my name was called and I walked over to a middle-aged woman in a bland dress whose lacquered hair was piled into a bee hive. She asked if there was an error about the three hours. "You mean thirty hours," she asked, pointing to my application. "No, you see, this T.A.-ship was a class in remedial English and we met only three times a week," I explained to her. She studied my face, pencil in her mouth and said, "Oh, I see." She wrote something on my application.

A few minutes later a business-type clapped his hands and announced that the applications would be processed and those whose work experience fitted their needs would be called. He said we could go home, and someone among the unemployable said: "Muther, you can go home!" The business-type pretended not to hear and walked away down the hallway.

Jon and I left laughing but were at once dazed by the heat and harsh light when we opened the outside door. It was late morning and already the day left us no choice: To stay inside in front of the air conditioner to nurse iced tea and a book that we hoped would never end.

My first book came out in March and Carolyn planned a party in June. A book-selling party. Carolyn stirred up a minor invasion of colorful dishes: Fruit platter, shrimp salad, and party-time meatballs. Then there were bowls of potato chips and guacamole. A few bottles of Wente chablis were chilled for a toast and beers were iced in a tub.

We spent the day rearranging the house. We scooted the

couch against the front window to face a small handsome Japanese print. We wiped the leaves of our three or four house plants, and cleaned the windows both inside and out. The bathroom was scrubbed, the floor vacuumed, and the living room scented with cut flowers from Carolyn's mother, an amateur flower arranger.

By seven the first guests began to arrive, some in pairs and others alone, but all were awkwardly quiet at first because few had been to a book-selling party and didn't know what to expect and because few had seen Carolyn and me in nine months—or years! Most guests were my relatives: brothers, sister, mother, aunt, uncles, cousins, and would-be cousins. Even my grandmother came with a cigarette in her shaking hand, and repeated in her gravelly voice all night: "Honey, your hair, your hair is too long!"

Then there were my literary companeros: Jon Veinberg and Leonard Adame. I handed out beers like tickets, and they were on their way to laughter and their overblown stories.

I had also invited my former teachers, Philip Levine and Peter Everwine, and they arrived with their wives and a well-known poet who had just ended a visiting professorship at Fresno State. The well-known poet shook my hand and retreated with Levine to take up a wine glass. Later, when Leonard Adame went up to ask about his translations from the Spanish, the well-known poet didn't feel much like talking. He answered Leonard's questions as simply as he could and then turned away to search out Levine.

By eight the party was loudly clever with reminiscences about my childhood. My mother: "Remember when this kid used to go raking leaves and he went up to one house and asked this lady—Armenian, I think—if she had any work to do and the lady says, 'Yes, I have to do the ironing and cook dinner,' and this kid don't know what to do except say 'Oh' and turn around and get his little butt off her porch. M'ijo, you crack me up."

By his third beer, my older brother started in: "And remember when he was in kindergarten I told him that peanut butter was also shoe polish? So he buffed it into his loafers and took off to school smelling like a sandwich. Gary, I'm sorry; I had to do it. You were so stupid."

They were stories dragged from the closet, stories that were a tradition at family gatherings, especially at Christmas when they nailed my brother to the wall, reminding him of the year he tore small holes in his Christmas presents to see what they were and later, on Christmas Eve, cried because none of them was a surprise.

I laughed along, although I tried unsuccessfully to change the subject. Carolyn finally intervened to ask if this knot of relatives would be interested in buying a copy of my book. My relatives flew to their purses and brought out their wallets. I signed books and tried to explain the poems at which most of them would only stare. They were very proud.

It was while signing books and making up stories about how I composed each poem in a blaze of concentration that my sister Debra tugged me into the bedroom where she pointed out the window at a young woman on top of the tin shed in the back yard. The woman was cursing at a young man who was waving a steak knife at her. He cursed at her and she returned even more fierce words about his and everyone else's mother.

They were a redneck-looking couple who lived in the apartment whose brick wall was a tall fence to our yard. A week before, while we were barbecuing with another couple, the woman's voice lifted almost beautifully from a high window, "Charlie, this new Tide even gets the shit out of your shorts," just as we were sitting down to eat and toast the good life.

Pulling down the shade, I felt inclined to telephone the police. I hesitated, however, and went over to tell Carolyn about what was happening outside. She rushed to the bedroom window and peeked through the shade. They were gone. Only the tin shed and the scraggly tomatoes.

My sister again tugged at my sleeve to whisper that the girl was at the front door. I scooted quickly past my guests, who were oblivious to what was going on, to answer the door. Calmly I answered, "Yes," searching her face for a clue to her feelings. She asked if she could use the phone because her car had broken down. I stared at her openly but her eyes refused to meet mine, even when I swung the door open and showed her to the phone. I left her alone but waited not far from her wondering if I should be direct and tell her that it wasn't a stalled car that brought her to my door but a steak knife. I didn't want to embarrass her, but I felt she must have been crumbling inside and was in need of comfort.

But I said nothing, for fear of getting involved, and when the young woman was off the telephone I walked her to the door and—very stupidly—wished her luck in getting her car started. On the steps she half-turned to me and looking at a cockroach that had scuttled out from the porch, said, "Thanks."

The party was a success. I sold twenty-two books and received many handshakes and loud cheers.

Short Takes

to Carolyn

Last night Ernesto, Dianne, and I sat at the dining table playing cards and drinking while Banjo went from one to another licking us. Poor dog, all day he was locked in the third bathroom because Ernesto had relatives over and, as you know, he has that nasty habit of pissing on the feet of strangers. Reluctantly, Ernesto had lured Banjo into the bathroom with a handful of dog chow. He leapt up amazingly high for such an old dog as he followed Ernesto's open palm with its gritty treasure. He made eating noises behind the door, then scratched to be let out, whined, and barked something like, "Come on, come on"—two syllable bursts that went unheeded, although I did slip a piece of meat under the door and wiggled my fingers for him to sniff and remember me.

We played cards, drank, and later watched Johnny Carson until the electricity failed. We lit candles just to see one another. The night sky helped out now and then with blue cracks of lightning. We told jokes—or more accurately—I told jokes and Ernesto and Dianne made sounds that could be considered laughter. Eventually Dianne, flushed from wine and wobbly as a restaurant chair, excused herself and went to bed while Ernesto stayed and begged me to go on—Ernesto, the most polite person I have ever met. Such sweetness. But finally he, too, trudged off to bed and I, not quite through with the night, went out onto the balcony to look at the roofs of other houses where I imagined laughter was breaking like the sea with every joke, funny or not.

And what did I do today? I woke very slowly with a book, had eggs and coffee, and went to work with Ernesto who wanted me to help translate some speeches of Portillo—speeches that he's going to give at the United Nations. They were all about oil: Oil and the Third World Countries, Oil and the Coming Years, Oil's Technological Prophecy, etc. But first we stopped off at the pharmacy near the *panaderia,* where I got an injection of penicillin. I've had a sore throat the last few days and have been tired. It wasn't my idea but Ernesto's. He's at the pharmacy all the time—or so the woman behind the counter mentioned with a tsk tsk. She waited on a boy who couldn't decide on Life Savers or cough drops before she waved me into the back room where I was asked to drop my pants as she searched, on tip toes, among a row of tiny boxes for the penicillin. Before she found it a customer called her away and I was left with my pants down, feeling ridiculous. She returned and searched some more among the boxes. When she found the penicillin she poked a needle into the bottle, shook it with a shiver of her wrist, and then turned to me, shooing her hand at me to bend over. "*Mas, joven! Mas, mas,*" she scolded me like a mother. I bent over until my shirt raised like a curtain, revealing my birthmark—that pirate's patch on the left cheek—and felt the sting.

When we got to the office Ernesto greeted his workers with smiles and handshakes, introducing me as a poet and professor. They shook my hand stiffly then stepped back with nods of respect that embarrassed me. He showed me the office where we would work. It looked out on that busy street where we once shopped for shoes. Ernesto left the room and returned with a folder under his arm. He took a seat, opened the folder on the coffee table, and began work by giving me a rough (but sometimes very accurate) translation of one of the speeches. At first we worked faithfully with the original but after awhile we got so sloppy we added words and phrases that weren't there and crossed out pretentious quips about how the poor, the noble Mexican poor, are the promise for the future. The speeches were real; they had been delivered in small towns on the frontier or in the interior while he was campaigning for the presidency. The rumor is that the mayor of each town had the streets swept, store fronts painted, and the terribly poor run into the countryside, before Portillo stepped off the plane and rode down an avenue lined with rouged girls who flung rose petals on tip toes.

We worked for five hours before we sent out for a pizza, only to return and make up some more speeches.

The day before you left, while you were out shopping for lacquerware at the national museum, I carried Mariko the five blocks to Chapultepec Park, past that pudgy policeman who usually whispers, "Here he comes, that young Mexican with his Chinese baby." He said it again to the hangers-on at the corner, and I smiled at him, then at Mariko, and crossed the street into the park looking for a quiet place to sit. But there wasn't any such place. If there weren't lovers pressed to trees, then there were kids with balloons or bright candies in their hands. If there weren't students from the Instituto Arquitectura talking in their sing-song voices, then there were cars honking, tinny transistors, and laughter from distant rowboats.

We finally stopped at a felled tree, a relief to my arms, and I let Mariko crawl in the grass and jab ants with a stick, her drool confusing them as they raced hysterically to get out of the way. Some got away, but some just kicked their feet in her drool, utterly bewildered I suppose at what was happening to them. She played happily with a handful of grass as I thought about her, how when we first arrived in Mexico her skin broke into a rash: Banjo nuzzled and licked her neck, and so started the rash that started the eczema that spread like fire and, I imagine, was a fire that she hoped to stop by scratching. But the eczema spread, some patches breaking with pus. You washed them daily, rubbed ointment the doctors prescribed, and still they teared like the eyes of small children. But the pain was ours, not really hers, because in a way she was like those ants—alive but not fully aware. At fourteen months she was only confused at why she hurt at her ankles, knees, elbows. Years from now she won't remember the pain that kept her up that one night crying but wanting so badly to be happy that she clapped patty-cakes, her face smeared with tears and snot. Remember? I rocked her at the dining table as you tried to sing, coo, and clap her into happiness.

At the park I let her crawl with those harmless ants. Later in a rented rowboat we drifted like so many others while Mariko greedily sucked a snow cone, something I shouldn't have bought for her but did anyway. From there we took a taxi home, but instead of going inside I carried her around the block, bouncing her quietly in my arms as I told her how I was going to miss her,

how I loved her. She smiled, made noises. She played with a
button on my shirt, squirmed to be let down, and said "flower,"
a new word for her, when she saw a balloon in a child's hand.
"Flower, flower," she said, legs kicking with happiness. Not a
bad guess, for such a little one.

Today I met with Carmen to practice Spanish. Afterward I
went alone to the Restaurante Gato Azul. Do you remember the
place? I went there once with Dianne's family who were shocked
when, after a graceful lunch of soup, sopa, and steak, the
waitress hurried over with the bill, pulling out bananas from her
pocket as she came. She offered them as dessert and, not
knowing what to do, we took the bananas and held them like
candles. Feeling silly, we peeled them and ate them with big
smiles. This afternoon I had custard for dessert. Later I walked to
the Biblioteca Benjamin Franklin where I looked at magazines
and at people, mostly Americans but some Japanese, who came
and went with anchors of books under their arms. Some looked
so happy and so bright that you could read from their exuberant
faces, while others were gray, disheveled, and sad as crushed
hats. But I found it difficult to concentrate, so I slouched in the
chair, eyes closed, and tried to recall something beautiful, like an
aria or our old apartment in Laguna Beach. I rested my eyes,
then left the library and walked toward the Metro, stopping
occasionally to look into shop windows, since I had time to kill
and the rains would not start for another hour.

At home I opened a beer and joined Dianne at the table where
she was playing cards and nursing a glass of wine. We played
solitaire and talked, first about Lindsay, her hometown, and then
ways to make money. A restaurant, we first said. Something in
Iowa City, where the bored were as numerous as corn. But we
figured it would be too much work, though we were on the right
track, since most people make their best decisions with their
mouths, not their minds. Ernesto came home, beautiful as ever in
his tailor-made suit, and joined us at the table. He suggested that
we make popsicles, natural ones filled with slices of banana and
apple, pinches of coconut, juices squeezed from real fruit. He
told us how his uncle in Mexicali once made and sold popsicles.
As a kid he'd sit on top of his uncle's truck and call out,
"Helados, muy deliciosos helados," to the kids who were, no

doubt, like those from my own childhood: Brown, skinny, and
crowned with spiky hair. So we talked and made sense; with beer
and friends things are so clear that wealth is possible, even in the
abstract. We could sell what we know, and isn't that what I am
doing now, teaching I mean. A few books read, some theory or
other dissolved like sugar in your speech, and you're pushed in
front of a classroom where students believe at least half of what
you say.

The truth is, I am unsure about where we will be in a year and
what life we will wake up to; we've had close calls in the past
when our passbook read close to zero. Anything is possible. Just
a few days ago, while I was walking Banjo, I saw a mother and
daughter who were absolutely filthy and in rags not even the
dead would wear. They were walking up the street, with mother
carrying a sack of things and the daughter with a soiled blanket
across her shoulder. They were not your typical Mexican poor
because their clothes were, from what I could tell, once
fashionable, once in style. The mother had on a polyester
pantsuit and the daugher wore a mini skirt and red patent pumps
that were cracked like mirrors. They passed me without looking
up and made their way to the end of the block only to look left
and then right, and then started back up the street. When they
passed me again, the girl's face met mine and I saw a fear so great
that it made me step back. I was shaken because they seemed so
average, in both looks and dress (if their clothes had been clean
and less tattered) and in most ways aren't we average? If poverty
could happen to them, then are we far behind from that day
when we'll carry all our belongings in a sack and call a blanket in
a doorway our bed? When we look up, we'll have the power to
make people step back.

We drank and talked. The way to make money is by way of
the palate, or so we think.

Remember my jacket, the leather one the Guggenheim people
paid for? A Mexican cop is wearing it today, feeling perhaps
handsome and smug at a street corner in this crazy city. It's gone,
that fine jacket that smelled of ham and was so unhumanly new.

Late yesterday Carmen and I had beers and taquitos at the
restaurant in Chapultepec Park, where we talked in English (it
was her day to practice). Afterward we returned to her car and

were about to drive away when a man stepped up to the car window, knocked on the glass, and held up his wallet for us to look at. Carmen rolled down the window to ask, *Que paso?* He said he was a policeman and that he wanted to warn us that there were thieves in the park, especially at night, and that we had better leave. But not before we proved, of course, that we were not thieves ourselves. He asked for the car registration, then Carmen's license. When I showed him my license he stopped chewing his gum as he read my name, street, and give-away-state, California. He looked down at me, eyes narrowing like a dog's, and began very quietly to accuse me of "eating" cocaine.

"*Los californios son 'jipis' y jotos, no?*" he said.

I tried to be jolly as a good friend of his, and I told him that he was mistaken, that we had had a few beers but most certainly not cocaine. He accused me of smoking marijuana, of being a hippie. Suddenly he pulled a gun from his waist, shaking it and ordering me out of the car. Carmen stiffened with anger and I got out without saying anything. The cop came around, yelled at me to place my hands on the hood and spread my legs, and it was like a scene from a movie made for TV. He patted my jacket and pants and then pushed me in the direction of his car where the door opened and a fat, very fat, cop got out with a taped stick.

When he said,"*Cabron*, we're going to do what American cops do to our people," I knew I was really in trouble. The one cop with the gun drove like a maniac through the park. Fat Guy took my wallet, which he greedily opened like a sandwich, and pulled out pesos and credit cards and even my library card—anything that looked like money to him. I emptied my pockets and handed over comb, Chiclets, and metro tickets. When he ordered me to pull down my pants, I played dumb and shrugged my shoulders. But that didn't help. He poked my stomach with his stick. Screamed: "*Andale, pinche cabron. Jipi shit!*"

I unbuckled my pants to show him that I wasn't hiding anything there. Disappointed, he made me roll up my sleeves, unbutton my shirt, and take off my shoes and socks. A real thorough guy. He even tousled my hair to see if I was concealing money up there.

By then we were driving up Reforma where we stopped for a few minutes at a corner that was so gaudy with neons and

Christmas lights it was like a poor man's fair. And the poor were there, along with children and the crippled selling lottery tickets, flowers, cough drops, peanuts, and balloons. Fat Guy got out to talk to someone at a *taqueria*, then got back in. We drove from there to a residential area, Lomas from what I could tell.

I was scared because I thought they were going to shoot me. A routine bang in the head. I was shaking and thinking of you and Mariko, forever gone, as I waited for something to happen. What happened was that Fat Guy asked me to turn my pockets inside out. He grabbed my jacket, which I gladly took off, and searched the pockets. Again he was disapointed. He crumbled it on his lap and turned to the driver. They spoke softly as drunken priests and, without warning, screeched the car to a halt, throwing me almost into the front seat. I was ordered out of the car with no fanfare or final threats, though I did have to jump back when the car revved its engine and roared away. I walked backward, almost on my heels, feeling so relieved that I thought I was a reborn Catholic.

I walked for a while, giddy with life for you and Mariko, before I flagged down a taxi and made it home to kick off my shoes, open a beer, and sit in the dining room with Ernesto and Dianne, to again turn over ideas about making money without so much as leaving the apartment.

A Good Day

Once, when we were bored and irritable in our apartment in Mexico City, the four of us—Ernesto, Dianne, Carolyn and I—got into the Renault we had bought the previous week and risked the rough and sometimes unfair roads that wound to Cuernavaca. We were happy in the car when we left and happier when we drove into town and discovered a fuchsia-like vine with red-flamed flowers. Carolyn took pictures of the vine from the car window—a vigorous vine that seemed to grow everywhere, on the houses of the poor as well as the rich. Dianne remarked it was the most beautiful flower she had ever seen.

We had lunch and lingered over dark beers, comfortable in the warm sunlight that slanted through an open window. We walked the *zocalo* where we bought trinkets from a child and visited a small museum in which the most interesting display was of rusted pistols and the sepia-colored photographs of those who had owned—or were killed by—the pistols. From there we went shopping: Dianne bought a belt for her niece and Carolyn turned over for the longest time silver charms that she hoped to add to a bracelet back in California. She chose an Italian flag and, with Dianne's help, argued over the price with the young woman behind the counter.

After shopping we drove outside the city in search of a nursery, to make our apartment more lush since it was uncomfortably bare: A dining table with chairs, an empty bird cage, two mattresses, and an ironing board that doubled as a writing table. We found a nursery and Ernesto and I haggled over ferns. In the end we paid what was asked and paid again when a boy helped us prop the plants in the trunk.

At the suggestion of a schoolgirl who had watched us shove and twist and grunt the plants into place, we drove further along the road to a pond that was pressed small by an arena of jagged rocks and wispy trees that were filled with birds. We walked along a leaf-littered path, paired off into couples looking very much like the tourists we were, until we were in view of divers approaching onlookers for a few pesos. We stopped and leaned against a stone fence, first to take pictures of the divers, and then of one another gazing into the distance, in the mock concentration of would-be free thinkers. Finally one diver who had counted and recounted his money stepped out onto a rock that jutted over the water. He took a deep breath, then released it. He took another deep breath, spread his arms, and leaped into the gray water that broke white as his body hit the surface. He came up smiling and pinching his nostrils. The onlookers clapped and smiled at one another.

We walked slowly back to the car, none of us looking forward to the drive back to the city, especially since the afternoon rains would soon start, so instead we started on a walk that ended only twenty feet from the car. Ernesto pointed to a harp player, a blind man who was very handsome in a felt hat and a crisp, white shirt. We walked in his direction behind Ernesto who, after a few minutes of casual remarks about the day, struck up a conversation that led to how the man had come to play the harp.

The story was that a group of Indians had come upon the wooden harp, stringless and warped, on a river bank. They turned it over in their hands for a long time but couldn't figure out what it was. Intrigued by this piece of wood, they carried it from the river up some difficult hills and into their village. One of the men carried it on his shoulder, like a slain deer. He was first greeted by children, then women, then the other men, and finally the head of the tribe who, baffled almost to the point of worry, banged at it with his fist. That night talk filled the air. Some said it was a suitcase. Others said it was a boat for very small children, and still others argued it was a loom. One said it was a washboard. Still they couldn't decide, so the three men who had found the harp took it back into town to sell it. But no one was interested in that piece of wood.

"But when they came to me, I knew what it was," he said.

"When I was a child in Morelia, my uncle played one, a very beautiful one inlaid with ivory and all glittery. That's when I could see and didn't need these hands."

He went on to tell us how the Indians had laid the instrument on his lap and he had run his hands over its body, recognizing it immediately but not revealing his happiness because it would have meant a difficult barter. After a few minutes of friendly haggling, the Indians walked into the countryside and up the hills with a frying pan and pocket knife, very pleased with the trade.

"Young man, I'll play for you—and for your friends of course," he said, wetting his lips and propping the harp against his shoulder. "It's a love song—*Mariposa en la primavera*." His fingers started slowly, like the butterflies of spring, but soon they plucked vigorously at the strings. He stopped once to cough into his sleeve and another time to wipe his brow, pausing for such a long time that we thought he had forgotten we were there. But he continued and when he finished we clapped and could think of no finer music as we looked at one another, moved by the song and this man who seemed so innocent despite his age. We thanked him and, as we were leaving, Ernesto tried to give him a few pesos. He refused them with a wave of his hand, "It's nothing, young man. Be a Mexican and go on."

We returned to the car, paired in couples and kicking at leaves and thinking how lucky we were. I started to hum. Ernesto joined in, and our wives pushed us away to cover their ears and make faces. We hummed louder, but when they picked up handfuls of leaves and twigs to throw at us, we stopped and mockingly opened our arms to them. Leaves fluttered in the air, and we chased them humming all the way down the hill to the car.